THE AESTHETIC FIELD
A Phenomenology of Aesthetic Experience

Publication Number 774
AMERICAN LECTURE SERIES®

A Monograph in
The BANNERSTONE DIVISION *of*
AMERICAN LECTURES IN PHILOSOPHY

Edited by
MARVIN FARBER
State University of New York at Buffalo
Buffalo, New York

THE AESTHETIC FIELD

A Phenomenology of Aesthetic Experience

By

ARNOLD BERLEANT, Ph.D.

Associate Professor of Philosophy
C. W. Post College of Long Island University
Brookville, New York

CHARLES C THOMAS • PUBLISHER
Springfield • Illinois • U.S.A.

Published and Distributed Throughout the World by
CHARLES C THOMAS • PUBLISHER

Bannerstone House
301-327 East Lawrence Avenue, Springfield, Illinois, U.S.A.
Natchez Plantation House
735 North Atlantic Boulevard, Fort Lauderdale, Florida, U.S.A.

© *1970, by* CHARLES C THOMAS • PUBLISHER
Library of Congress Catalog Card Number: 72-97543

With THOMAS BOOKS *careful attention is given to all details of
manufacturing and design. It is the Publisher's desire to present books
that are satisfactory as to their physical qualities and artistic possibilities
and appropriate for their particular use.* THOMAS BOOKS *will be true
to those laws of quality that assure a good name and good will.*

Printed in the United States of America
W-13

PREFACE

THE RANGE OF ART has changed radically in recent years. Not only has it widened to include objects that once seemed totally foreign to anything artistic, but it has also become more difficult to separate the fine from the practical arts, for functional considerations have infused both. Art, too, has tended to become socially involved in ways that extend far beyond the drawing room, and we are no longer able to keep our composure in the face of the involving, even inflammatory materials and methods of the modern arts.

Yet the boundaries of art have been extended vertically as well as horizontally. Instead of regarding art as the flower of civilization, we now see it as part of the very roots. It is not just that we have found in primitive art of the past and present a major source of new vitality in modern painting, sculpture, dance, and music. We have discovered that art of a high order appears in primordial societies and under the most primitive conditions of human life, rather than being the luxurious indulgence of wealth and ease. Indeed, the aesthetic impulse can be discerned in artifacts that date from the appearance of paleolithic man, as in the fascination with shapes in stone tools combined with a high degree of workmanship, in the patterns and designs in ivory engravings, and in the cave paintings at Lascaux and Altamira that date back 20,000 to 40,000 years. Artistic skill and aesthetic sensibility are no recent acquisitions.

Ancient, perhaps as ancient, are the origins of attempts to explain such activities. Mytho-religious at first, theories of the nature of art have come to abandon their animistic overtones and assume greater intellectual and abstract content. There has been no limit to ingenuity, and interpretations of art have covered the gamut from metaphysical revelations of Being, to cognitive theories of art as symbol, and hedonistic ones of art as pleasure. Moreover, the constant dissatisfaction with these

v

explanations not only shows that the phenomena of art allow widely differing interpretations; it also testifies to the lack of success in providing a sufficiently convincing account.

One of the principal difficulties with aesthetic theory has been its failure to respond sufficiently to the arts themselves. And as the arts have extended their range and become a pervasive force in modern life, traditional boundaries and restraints of aesthetics have become increasingly irrelevant. Aesthetic theory seems more at a loss than ever before to deal adequately with the challenge of artistic inventiveness.

Yet it is certainly not inevitable that theories of art must trail dismally behind the activity of art, or that they must change with the prevailing intellectual winds. What this may indicate is that aesthetic theory has failed so far to achieve the maturity and the intellectual autonomy of a developed cognitive discipline. By lending the charms of art to grace the fleshless forms of moral and metaphysical doctrines and of social and psychological theories, aesthetics has played a servile role; it has not done adequate justice to the significance of art in human experience.

The chapters that follow attempt to develop the main outlines of an aesthetic theory, one that tries to treat the problems of aesthetics freshly and without prior commitment to outside doctrines or systems. They are bound together by a common point of departure—the conviction that the roots of aesthetic theory must draw sustenance from the rich soil of aesthetic experience. This unifying theme is grounded in the belief that a genuinely empirical approach to aesthetics, an approach that up to now has never been systematically developed, offers the greatest promise of adequately accounting for a subject matter that is inherently experiential. I hope to show how a number of problems that have constantly troubled aesthetic theory can be clarified in the light of the theory that will be developed here.

The first chapter attempts to establish the cognitive respectability of aesthetics by determining the nature and role of aesthetic theory, the data on which it must be based, and the method by which it must be developed. The next chapter examines how the usual kinds of concepts and commitments have typically distorted aesthetics by acting as surrogates or inadequate substitutes for genuine explanations. Chapter III offers an alternative to such approaches by developing the notion of an aesthetic field, grounded on an analysis of the experiential matrix in which art and aesthetic perception occur. The following chapter explores the aesthetic mode of experience, tracing its implications for a number of common aesthetic problems and proposals. Chapter V extends the argument into the region of art criticism and lays the basis for an understanding of aesthetic value. Finally, Chapter VI brings together the themes of the preceding chapters and suggests some directions for future exploration.

The ideas that this book develops have a certain timeliness, for they can account remarkably well for much of what is happening in the contemporary arts. Yet their topical character was not calculated. The concept of the aesthetic field and its consequences for the philosophy of art began to emerge in my own thinking nearly six years ago, before I had the kind of modest acquaintance with the contemporary arts that I have since acquired. In refining this notion and applying it to the perennial problems of aesthetics, it became clear that the idea of the aesthetic field was able to accommodate artistic innovation and tradition with equal ease.[1] Yet rather than being the reason for developing the notion of the aesthetic field, this stands, I think, as a confirmation of it.

In any case, the arts contain a rich store of problems for philosophy. I hope that the ideas that this book develops can help in resolving many such issues, and that they will contribute toward constructing a theoretical framework in aesthetics that will rest on compelling evidence and justify common assent. While there is much here that is controversial, this is neither a merit nor a defect. I ask only that what I have written be judged in the light of the facts of aesthetic activity and not the conventions of aesthetic thought.

Glen Cove, New York   ARNOLD BERLEANT

---

[1] This book does not attempt to examine the contemporary arts as such. A somewhat historical analysis which explores the significant implications these arts hold for aesthetic theory can be found in my "Aesthetics and the Contemporary Arts," *J. of Aesthetics and Art Criticism,* forthcoming.

ACKNOWLEDGMENTS

AN AUTHOR'S INDEBTEDNESS in writing a work of this nature is always large, and covers everything but the limited range of his own originality. This book is no exception. It had its origins in a suggestion of my friend, former teacher and colleague, Professor Marvin Farber, and I gratefully acknowledge my deep indebtedness to him. Special thanks are due Professors John Peter Anton, Monroe Beardsley, and Allan Shields, all of whom read and commented upon portions of the manuscript. I have profited much from their scholarship and criticism. To my wife, Riva S. Berleant, I owe encouragement, patience, and a merciless editorial eye. Needless to say, the responsibility for whatever is debatable or infelicitous I take upon myself. I should like to thank, too, my former student Mary Woodward for a suggestion from which Figure 3 was adapted, and the editors of *Philosophy and Phenomenological Research* and the *Sarah Lawrence Journal,* respectively, for their kind permission to reprint materials in Chapters II and V which appeared there in earlier versions. I also want to express my appreciation to the administration of C. W. Post College of Long Island University for making time available for me to complete this project, and to the Research Committee for a grant to prepare the final typescript. Finally, no acknowledgment in a book of this sort would be complete without mentioning Thomas Munro, who has pointed the way to a naturalistic aesthetics and has surveyed the path we all must follow.

A. B.

CONTENTS

LIST OF ILLUSTRATIONS

THE AESTHETIC FIELD
A Phenomenology of Aesthetic Experience

I

AESTHETIC THEORY AS A COGNITIVE DISCIPLINE

SUPPOSED LIMITS OF KNOWLEDGE

Nowhere has it been so consistently difficult for men to agree as in discussions of art. Some, indeed, have regarded this difficulty with undisguised approval, seeing in it irrefutable testimony to the limitations of human knowledge. For here, they feel, in the realm of artistic activity, can man's spirit achieve untrammeled freedom, emancipated from the fetters of the scientific and the quotidian.

Yet such defensive anti-intellectualism adds nothing to the magnitude of man's creative achievements. Great art is made no greater by being inexplicable. Indeed, the belief that it is impossible to attain rational knowledge of art suggests a self-contradictory attitude—one that extolls human ingenuity while at the same time denies its power. For intellectual advance is also a profound achievement of the human spirit—to insist on the impossibility of understanding artistic activity is to parade a failing as a virtue.

Such claims that there are insurmountable barriers to inquiry have usually arisen from the fear that the light of knowledge might cause some cherished beliefs or institutions to wilt. The isolation of aesthetic and moral interests from rational inquiry is sometimes made to rest on supernatural or transcendental grounds, where it is often accompanied by a certain satisfaction in denying the primacy of human concerns in order to enforce man's subservience to some higher authority. These difficulties, however, rest on reasons other than those that lie in the task of understanding values. It is those who claim that there are limitations to understanding and that human existence must play a secondary role who must assume the burden of proof. We cannot demonstrate the impossibility of successful inquiry into human values, aesthetic and ethical, from general premises about the nature of man or the universe. Whatever tentative conclusions we can draw must be the outcome of careful, detailed investigation of the phenomena of valuing themselves. Abstract *a priori* principles have been notoriously unsuccessful in settling issues that concern matters of fact and experience.

At other times there have been elaborate efforts to draw lines between what men could successfully hope to understand and what lay beyond their comprehension. The Cartesian dualism of body and spirit, still very influential in aesthetic theory, had the intent of opening the full range of physical events to investigation and explanation by Newtonian physics, while pacifying religious fears that the human soul was being endangered by the constant encroachments of science. A similar instance was Kant's division of the world into the phenomenal realm of appearance, in which science revealed the operation of a causal order of necessary relations, and a noumenal realm of things-in-themselves, where God, freedom, and immortality were possible. Here, too, limits of knowledge were drawn in the hope of preserving the previously unknowable from the degradation of being explained.

Scientific inquiry, though, has overridden Descartes by moving beyond the physical to the psychical. And the dichotomy of Kant has not weathered the twin perils of the practical need that men be held responsible for the consequences of their actions, and the logical requirement that men not claim knowledge of what they have excluded as beyond the range of human experience. The demands of action and consistency are indeed dangers that beset the route of every philosophical conception, and they are the major correctives to an intellectual imagination that regards itself as self-sufficient. These holding actions, then, have been both conceptually unsuccessful and historically misguided. They have had to retreat continuously before the advances of biology, anthropology, psychology, and the other sciences of human behavior, and have been forced to regroup on new and more precarious intellectual ground.

All these outside influences, though, may account only in part for the failure of aesthetics to develop a body of commonly accepted theory. It may well be that there are difficulties in the subject matter of aesthetics itself that explain why it has not progressed beyond a speculative stage. These may be responsible for the failure of any single theoretical approach to gain general acceptance. It is on such grounds as these that the exclusion of aesthetics as a cognitive discipline has received unexpected support from recent movements in philosophy which associate themselves with scientific problems, procedures, and standards. The contemporary positivists in particular, by assigning non-cognitive status to the valuational content of normative judgments, have contributed to the exclusion of aesthetics as a legitimate, intellectual discipline. By barring the activities of art and the experience of beauty as fair game for the development of theory, and by denying the possibility of constructing conceptual standards of appraisal, the result in aesthetics, as in ethics, however unintentional, is to demean human understanding and to reinforce a convention that is often uncritical. Indeed, the logical positivists often impose more rigorous standards for aesthetic knowledge than they do for the established sciences.[1] In doing so, they not only ignore the significant achievements that have already been made by careful investigation; they

---

[1] A. J. Ayer, for example, has insisted that because it is not self-contradictory to deny ethical subjectivism or utilitarianism, these ethical philosophies must be rejected. Yet according to him, it is definitions which it should be self-contradictory to deny because they are tautologies. To insist that ethical utilitarianism meet the standard of definitions and not of empirical statements begs the question of what indeed they are. Why insist that ethical principles be tautologous while (other) empirical statements need not? To do so imposes so stringent a logical requirement on ethical statements that it prejudges them to be nonempirical and thus bound by formal logical requirements. And since they do not meet these requirements, they are consequently rejected as cognitively meaningful. If, however, such ethical principles were empirical generalizations verified by actual sense experience, they would then have to be admitted as cognitively significant. This is the point at issue, but Ayer does not resolve or even deal with it. He avoids doing so by assuming in advance the logical incompatibility of ethical and factual statements, and by imposing standards more rigorous for ethical statements than for admittedly empirical ones. The same objections apply, *mutatis mutandis,* to aesthetic statements. Cf. *Language Truth and Logic,* rev. ed. (London, 1946), pp. 94, 99, 104-5.

legislate as well against the future possibility of aesthetic knowledge.

Thus, in the manner of Kant, a new haven has now been discovered in the realm of values. Here man's spirit can freely move without the restraints that logic or practice would impose. While science dominates the universe of fact, values are non-natural or noncognitive, and thus beyond its reach. Art in particular supposedly benefits from this, on the ground that judgments of aesthetic value ultimately need answer to no one.

It is with methodological problems such as these that this chapter is concerned. If we wish to discover whether a cognitive aesthetics is possible, we must first clarify the nature and task of aesthetic theory. Then we can explore the method that is appropriate for constructing such a body of theoretical knowledge.

THE TASK OF AESTHETIC THEORY

It is, in general, the task of any theory to account for a set of phenomena, and by doing this, to make experience more understandable and, consequently, easier to achieve and control. The theorist is not attempting primarily to define concepts and construct systems. Rather, he is engaging in an effort to identify, relate, and explain phenomena, an effort which has its fruit in successful application. Theory therefore first examines those experiences that both attract and puzzle us, and defines the limits of discussion by the relevance of the phenomena to the initial problem. The theorist then develops concepts and discerns relationships. He elaborates the categories and structures that are most appropriate to the issues with which he is coping, to the data he is capable of acquiring, and by the success with which he can account for and control experience. Thus it is to experience that we first must turn, and it is experience which dictates the appropriate theoretical structures, meanings, and operations.

Aesthetic theory, in particular, has the task of accounting for aesthetic phenomena. Its purpose is to render more understandable the experiences of art and the aesthetic perception of nature. To do this satisfactorily, aesthetics must construct conceptual tools which derive directly from aesthetic experience. It must formulate ideas which return to clarify and enhance our future experience by helping us to recognize, order, and respond to it in ways that are appropriate to the phenomena. The pattern of inquiry in aesthetics, then, is no different from the pattern of inquiry in any other cognitive discipline. Thus the first task is to identify the boundaries of aesthetic experience, for this determines the range of aesthetic phenomena and the objects with which they are associated.

Here we stand at a crucial point in the process of inquiry about art. At this stage much theorizing about art makes a false step by taking as its *terminus a quo* a previously accepted body of art works whose choice predetermines the kind of conclusion to which one is led. Thus the proponents of imitation turn to representational works and then reject those that are abstract, while those who take a formalist position look to abstract art and ignore what is representational. We must, however, determine the objects of art by the experience of art, not the experience by the objects. For to do the latter begs the question of what is indeed artistic. Surely it is only on the basis of our perceptual encounter with them that we can decide what objects are aesthetic and why. When we reject art objects because they are made of discarded machine parts, magnetic tapes spliced together, pasted cutouts, and the like, we are inverting the empirical order of art and using the product to judge the perception instead of the perception the product. And often an implicit theory is dictating our decision *a priori*.

It is therefore essential for a genuinely empirical aesthetics to begin by acknowledging all the relevant phenomena, not by denying or excluding them. It must impartially consider the use of techniques, forms, styles and media which are commonly ridiculed, shrugged off, or relegated to the status of aberrations. These include such recent developments as moving sculpture, *objets trouvées*, collages, assemblages, pop art, op art, light shows, Happenings, theater-in-the-round, theater of the absurd, electronic music, aleatoric music, mixed media, and some of the more spectacular techniques of applying paint to canvas. A truly effective aesthetic theory must account for the history of artistic style, and for the facts that styles in art are constantly changing and that we are forever reappraising the different periods in the history of art. It must accept and explain cultural influences on the development of style and transcultural responses to art, such as the reactions of westerners to Indian music, Byzantine icons, and African drum patterns. Aesthetics must account for differences in the experience and judgment of practiced observers, and for the lack of universal agreement on the value of specific art works. It must acknowledge and explain the kind, degree, and variety of appeal that different genres of art possess, from popular and folk to classical and *avant garde*. It must also deal with the psychology of artistic creation in order to see how this can help us understand the phenomena of art. And finally, an empirical aesthetics must clarify the relationships between art and nature, technology and knowledge. It must account for the place of ideas in art and the relationship that art has to human beliefs and institutions.

Aesthetics thus embraces a wide range of data and problems. Yet while a sound theory must account for all of them, many aestheticians respond only by excluding and rejecting many of them. Theories of art, like formalism in painting, absolutism in music, and the New Criticism in literature, propose normative standards of what is relevant and what is not in aesthetic perception. Yet these standards do not derive from a careful examination of aesthetic data but rather from the very theories that are advanced to explain them. Such theories establish their own criteria for determining which objects are legitimately artistic, and buttress their positions by eliminating whatever evidence is contrary. One thinks here of those tendentious distinctions that writers often make, such as Véron's discrimination of expressive from decorative art, Tolstoy's real from counterfeit art, and Fry's pure from impure art. These distinctions allow the writer to select the data to fit his theory instead of adapting his theory to account for all the data.

There is no monopoly on legislative aesthetics. Traditionally-minded writers begin with some commonly accepted view and then seek to discredit new movements in art on the basis of that view. For example, critics of nonrepresentational styles in painting such as abstract expressionism, or styles like cubism and surrealism that employ a high degree of distortion, often appeal to the imitation theory to support their attacks. And champions of the *avant garde* often commit the identical error in reverse. They seize upon the innovations that previous theories cannot assimilate, and then develop a theory to justify them. While they may succeed in explaining these new developments, they usually find it difficult to account for the art from which earlier theories derived their support. This, for example, was the most striking shortcoming of formalism as a viable alternative to the imitation theory.

All these observations would be unnecessary were it not for the fact that they have regularly been ignored in the history of aesthetic thought, from imitation and emotionalism to formalism, symbolism, and expressionism. Yet this history can serve a valuable purpose by instructing us on the handicaps that partial data inflict on aesthetic theory, and it suggests the direction we should follow in avoiding them. Unfortunately, however, critics and philosophers have continued to treat aesthetic phenomena in an *a priori* fashion by tacitly assuming a theory of art, and then being guided by that theory rather than by the artistic data themselves. They have continued to accept common assumptions, which, however, do not accord with the data we possess. One such view is the belief that a valid aesthetic judgment must be universal, which carries the consequence either that disagreement is somehow the result of defective judgment or that universal judgment is impossible. (Compare this situation with that in scientific theory, where agreement and disagreement work in dialectical interplay in the ongoing process of investigation, and contribute to the constant improvement of both empirical knowledge and theoretical explanation.) Another assumption is the conviction that there is a qualitative difference between fine art and the popular or practical arts, and that the same aesthetic criteria do not apply.

The purpose of theory, however, is not to demonstrate that certain kinds of experiences and judgments associated with art are inadequate; it is rather to explain why they do in fact occur.

A genuine aesthetics should offer what is initially a phenomenological account. It must begin by being primarily descriptive
rather than judicial, and develop its normative standards from
an observational base. Rather than starting from *a priori*
standards of relevance and excellence, an empirical aesthetics
should try to identify such standards through a careful examination of the nature of aesthetic experience itself. Instead of
prejudging aesthetic phenomena by a theory accepted in advance,
the first step for a methodologically sound aesthetics is to identify
all the relevant phenomena. Moreover, the criteria of relevance
for the data of art are not established exclusively by a theory;
the standards must come rather from a close examination of the
independent evidence of the experience of art. It is necessary,
then, to acknowledge all the data associated with art and the
aesthetic, and to develop a theoretical explanation inductively
from them.

Thus the role of aesthetic theory is no different from what
it is in any other field of inquiry. Historical theory attempts to
account for historical events by discerning patterns and relationships, causes and consequences. Physical theory tries to explain
physical events by identifying lawful sequences and by ordering
the symbolic expression of them into formal structures. Psychological theory searches for the relevant influences on personality
development, learning behavior, motivation, and the like, and
seeks to identify causal relationships and developmental patterns.
As with these cognitive disciplines, so with aesthetics. Aesthetic
theory must deal wth aesthetic events by first identifying the
circumstances under which such events occur. Only then can
it clarify the interrelationships that hold among the creation,
the performance, and the appreciative perception of art. In
addition, aesthetics must examine the significance for aesthetic
perception of the various influences on artistic style, and explore
the connections that art objects have to other events in human
experience.

By referring to aesthetic phenomena, however, I am not
begging the question of what aesthetic theory must explain.
What I am doing is rather plotting out a region in the matrix
of human experience that is commonly distinguished from other

modes of experience. Just as it is possible to speak meaningfully of social, religious, technical, or sensory phenomena without having to adjudge the more ambiguous cases, so can we appeal to those aesthetic phenomena that men have commonly identified. It is these phenomena—the experiences of art and beauty that we have and acknowledge as such—that are the proper basis on which to develop our theoretical conceptions. Only by proceeding from this point can the boundaries of such experience be more sharply defined in the light of an adequate theoretical account.[2]

There is a considerable expanse of common ground on which most people involved with the arts stand together. This agreement is typically overshadowed by the more spectacular cases of controversy which make artistic news. Yet this consensus is of first importance in developing a sound theory of art. Thus there is a body of widely accepted critical judgment about particular objects in the different arts that corresponds to the accepted body of knowledge in other fields. Our Bachs, Rembrandts, and Shakespeares have achieved a stature that is essentially stable, even though our evaluations of individual works may occasionally vary. Granted there are heretics and dissenters from such prevailing judgments. Yet eccentricities of judgment occur in every area of scholarship and investigation; they are not peculiar to art. Moreover, these serve to discourage dogmatism and blind veneration, intellectual vices in any field.

In proceeding initially from the body of commonly accepted experience and judgment in art, we are merely following the successful precedent of the sciences. Historians of science have

---

[2] This is discussed more fully in Chapter IV. Cf. pp. 93-96.

Dewey insists that we go from the aesthetic in daily experience to the aesthetic in works of art. He rejects the compartmentalization and isolation of fine art from the body of human experience, and emphasizes that aesthetic characteristics may appear in all kinds of experience. Although I accept both of these views, to follow Dewey's course requires that we first stipulate the nature of aesthetic experience so that it can be recognized in ordinary experience. Yet doing this inverts the relation between aesthetic theory and other modes of experience, and begs the question of what the features of aesthetic experience are. The course I have followed here is less assumptive. I shall begin with a description of experience in the aesthetic situation and from this try to discern the aesthetic quality in other modes of experience.

observed that modern science began when men first studied the typical occurrences in nature rather than its more startling aberrations. Only when the patterns of common events were identified and formulated did it become possible to explain the so-called exceptions by the same laws, as special cases of the more usual. There is good reason, then, to hypothesize that it will be no different in aesthetics.

It would not be necessary to make these commonplace observations about agreement in aesthetic judgment but for the fact that it is often overlooked in preference to the sensationalism of flamboyant innovation and controversy. Yet such consensus has further relevance for aesthetic theory. For the fact of general critical agreement implies recognition of the aesthetic character of the experiences on which they are based. These are the circumstances in which people customarily engage in an aesthetic transaction, and it is these circumstances that are the point of departure of any aesthetic theory and the point of· return by which it must be tested.[3]

AESTHETIC FACTS

There is, indeed, a considerable store of perceptual experience that we generally regard as aesthetic. Just how to describe such experiences is an important question and one that will occupy us throughout the rest of this book. Yet our concern at this stage is not primarily with the content of aesthetic theory but rather with the method that must be followed in constructing a viable explanation. Once we have identified the phenomena of aesthetic experience, what kinds of facts—aesthetic facts—

----

[3] The limits of such circumstances may be widened to admit experiences outside the bounds of the artistic which have commonly been observed to be similar. These include the aesthetic qualities of mathematical demonstration and of natural objects, from the homely field flower to the cascading waterfall and towering mountain range. Ideas, too, may be taken aesthetically, for there is the quasi-perceptual intellectual illumination that cognitive insight can bring. Whether such circumstances as these can be included is, of course, more debatable than the conventionally artistic. And whether one can rightly regard them as aesthetic can only be decided after achieving an acceptable theory using more typical instances.

can we hope to accumulate which a theory must unify and explain? By facts I do not mean the events or occurrences which involve art and beauty, but rather highly probable *statements* about these events, especially general statements, that have been arrived at by carefully examining those situations in which aesthetic phenomena occur. These are the facts of aesthetic experience and not of aesthetic theory, but they are the ground out of which aesthetic theory must grow.

What do such facts comprise? There are at least five distinguishable kinds:

1. *Situational Facts.* First there are those statements that describe *the conditions under which aesthetic experience occurs.* These claim to identify the factors that are present when people are aesthetically occupied. Such statements include descriptions of aesthetic appreciation as disinterested or distanced, or of the aesthetic situation as involving one with the sensible qualities of objects, or of the aesthetic attitude as a sympathetic openness to the object.

2. *Experiential Facts.* Then there are statements that presume to describe *the characteristics of aesthetic experience* itself. These derive from the accounts of qualified perceivers, such as creative and performing artists, practiced observers, critics, and psychologists. Such descriptions of aesthetic experience attempt to identify its chief characteristics and to distinguish it from other modes of experiences, such as the practical and cognitive. They include such common accounts of aesthetic experience as Vernon Lee's notion of empathy when the activities of the perceiver tend to merge with the qualities of the object, or Ogden, Richards, and Wood's contention that the experience of beauty is a state of synaesthesis, in which we experience the impulses that art arouses in a harmonious way without any tendency to action.

3. *Objective Facts.* Next there are statements about *the objects which are involved in aesthetic experience* and which are the central focus of our attention. It is here that questions arise about the aesthetic relevance of the various features of art objects, such as their formal and material traits, about the significance of stylistic innovations in the arts, and about the

aesthetic interest of commonplace, practical, and natural objects and events.

4. *Judgmental Facts.* Then there is *the body of critical judgments about these objects and events.* These incorporate the valuational experience of an art public. They express the normative conclusions that have emerged from considerable exposure and discussion of art objects, styles, and media.

5. *Interdisciplinary Facts.* Finally there are those facts that have resulted from *studies of aesthetic events and objects from the standpoint of various related disciplines.* Aesthetic events form the data from which we are able to make verifiable generalizations and predictions about the individual and social psychology of aesthetic experience, the sociology of aesthetic activities like the performance, criticism, and institutions of art, cultural influences on aesthetic experience, historical trends in style, material, performance, and the like.

Because aesthetic facts rest on empirical data, they are capable of empirical confirmation. Yet there are obvious difficulties that lie in the way of accumulating such facts, and the examples I have given are not immune to these. There is the need to become clearer about the aesthetic phenomena on which they are grounded. There is also the need to identify and obtain these different sorts of factual statements. A prior difficulty, however, results from the ways in which nonaesthetic considerations have constantly determined aesthetic theory. Theory in aesthetics has rarely been developed in independent terms. Beliefs in aesthetics have been dictated instead by particular moral standards which are used to decide on the acceptability of everything from subject matter and form to vocabulary and costume. Sometimes the nature of theory has been determined by the requirements for completeness and order that are imposed by religious commitments, or by a philosophical system like that of Kant. And often social practices and cultural traditions have imposed standards for particular art forms, media, and styles.

What is certain, however, is that for aesthetics to meet its theoretical goals adequately, it must develop as an autonomous discipline. It must obtain its own data, formulate observed regularities into factual statements, and construct a theoretical framework capable of empirical verification which will both guide such research and organize its results. Whether or how moral, religious, metaphysical, social, or cultural considerations are relevant can only be decided after the typically aesthetic has been identified, described, and explained, and not in advance.

The accumulation of aesthetic facts has proceeded at a slow rate, and considerably more research is necessary. It is here that a clear awareness of method in aesthetics can help. For an empirical aesthetics can proceed soundly only on the basis of such facts as these. It can neither ignore nor assume them; rather it should attempt to develop a unified explanation of them. As the body of factual knowledge increases in quantity and accuracy, aesthetic theory will also have to develop and change. Only through such a procedure as this can aesthetics really assume the character of a respectable cognitive discipline and achieve a body of knowledge that can demand our acceptance. Only in this way, too, will aesthetics be able to function as a guide to the full development of our artistic resources.

THE METHOD AND STRUCTURE OF AESTHETIC THEORY

We are now in a position to summarize the results of this discussion and to suggest how aesthetic theory should proceed. As a cognitive discipline, aesthetics must begin by focusing on the body of aesthetic experience that we can identify as a determinable mode in the matrix of human activity. Because of the biosocial nature of human experience, it is possible to build on common ground by acquiring a body of data that can function as common evidence. On the basis of such evidence we can hope to establish a collection of aesthetic facts on which to obtain a reasonable consensus. Such common evidence and accepted fact provide the material from which to construct a general theory of aesthetics, one that can claim broad acceptance. Figure 1 schematizes these relationships.

Since it has developed out of aesthetic experience, an empirical aesthetics can hope to arrive at verified explanations of such experience. It will be capable of identifying the conditions

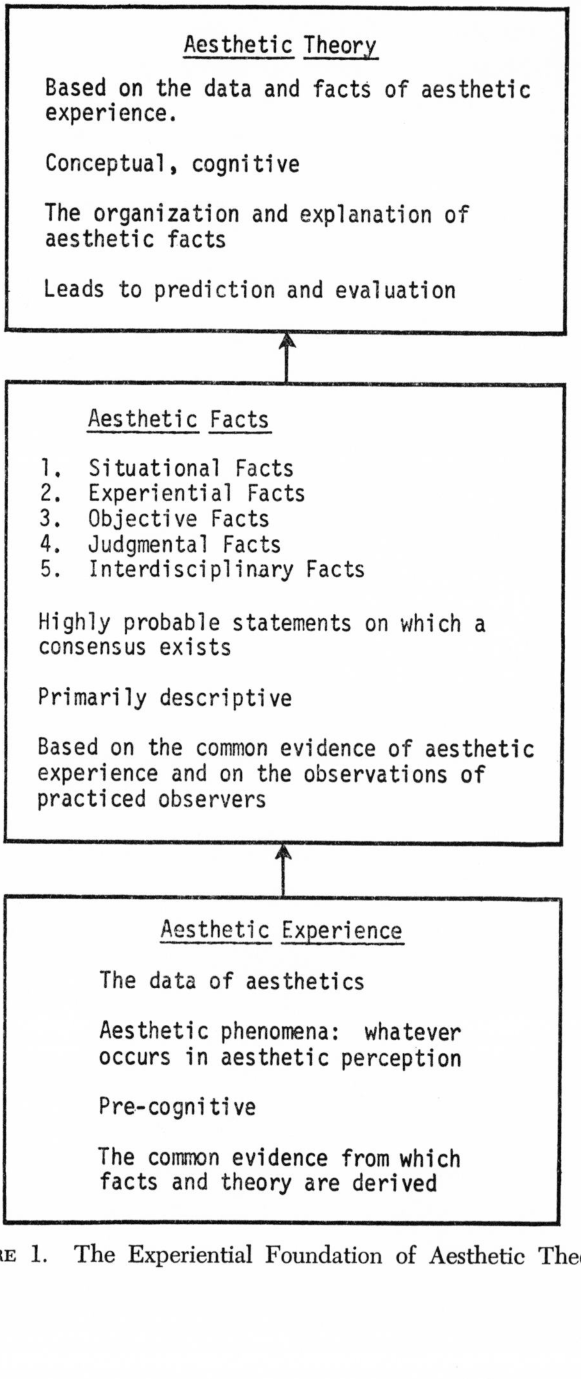

Aesthetic Theory

Based on the data and facts of aesthetic experience.

Conceptual, cognitive

The organization and explanation of aesthetic facts

Leads to prediction and evaluation

Aesthetic Facts

1. Situational Facts
2. Experiential Facts
3. Objective Facts
4. Judgmental Facts
5. Interdisciplinary Facts

Highly probable statements on which a consensus exists

Primarily descriptive

Based on the common evidence of aesthetic experience and on the observations of practiced observers

---

Aesthetic Experience

The data of aesthetics

Aesthetic phenomena: whatever occurs in aesthetic perception

Pre-cognitive

The common evidence from which facts and theory are derived

FIGURE 1. The Experiential Foundation of Aesthetic Theory.

of aesthetic experience, its characteristics, and its internal and external relationships. Aesthetic theory can also provide a basis on which to make informed predictions about the effects of changes in conditions on aesthetic experience, the manner in which artistic innovations will be received and accepted, and the effectiveness of various techniques in educating people in the appreciation of art objects. Further, a general theory of aesthetics will also proceed to develop standards for appraising art objects on cognitive grounds. Once we recognize that aesthetic theory emerges out of aesthetic experience, it is but a short step to realizing that the test of accuracy and adequacy for aesthetic theory lies in its ability to return us to aesthetic experience clarified, enlightened, and with enhanced potential for perception. It is in view of this goal that normative judgment in aesthetics becomes cognitive. If aesthetic theory begins and ends in experience, it is not only possible to verify the theory by the adequacy of its explanations. It also becomes possible to develop standards for judging specific art objects by their role in facilitating and enhancing aesthetic experience. This suggestion will be taken up in a later chapter.

Method in aesthetics, then, becomes the procedures by which we collect the data of aesthetics, arrive at probable statements, and develop theoretical explanations, predictions, and standards of judgment. It is, in short, the way of working on aesthetic experience in order to attain knowledge. While we can readily describe the outlines of the course to be followed, the full development and application of a general theory of aesthetics is a task that requires the cooperative efforts of many investigators. Much has already been done, to be sure. While there are already areas of agreement in some categories of aesthetic facts, there remains a lack of clarity about the conditions and characteristics of aesthetic experience. As a consequence, theoretical concepts and structures have not yet developed adequately.

The role of philosophy here, then, is limited. Philosophy is not an empirical science, and it is not suitably equipped to accumulate and test facts. It can, however, perform the important tasks of identifying difficulties which beset aesthetic theory and clarifying the issues at stake. Philosophy can also contribute to our methodological awareness and to our organization of the materials of aesthetic theory. It is programmatic as well, setting forth the conditions for successful investigation and suggesting directions for inquiry.

The purpose of this study, then, is twofold. It is first to propose an account of aesthetic experience. This, however, cannot be done without pointing out the shortcomings of commonly held theories which do not accurately describe it. Second, it is to relate this account of aesthetic experience to theory by suggesting suitable concepts, categories, and standards of relevance by which such an empirically grounded theory can proceed. All these analyses and proposals are tentative and corrigible. They are meant to provide a beginning for the eventual development of a general theory of aesthetics, one that can command the same widespread acceptance as other cognitive disciplines have attained.

II

SURROGATE THEORIES OF ART

Anyone who begins the study of aesthetics is likely to be overwhelmed by the diversity of theories men have devised to interpret their experiences of art. It would seem that art means different things to different people, and that there is as little agreement on what art is as there is on the standards by which art is to be judged. Moreover, these two problems are not unrelated, for the lack of success in resolving the one has contributed to the failure in devising a solution to the other. Because of such widespread lack of accord, it might appear as if any attempt to say something new on the subject would be doomed in advance to the limbo of arbitrary opinion.

Consider the variety of proposals that have already been made. Art, according to some, is an attempt to represent, through the use of a sensuous medium, the actual or ideal, the things we perceive or the underlying nature of reality, by imitating their appearance or their formal structure. Others view art subjectively as the manifestation of pleasure or emotion. At times art is interpreted as psychic symbol; at other times it is seen as the symbol of feeling. It has been construed as a mode of expression, and it has been rendered as a special language through which communication can take place. It is a free, self-gratifying activity resembling play, the manifestation of the inner workings of the universal Will, or direct, intuitive vision. Moreover, each theory purports to give an exclusive and comprehensive account of what art is; each seizes upon undeniable features of art and casts them into a meaningful mold. It would appear almost as if the laws of logic were suspended, and that all the explanations, however incompatible with one another, were collectively true.

Actually, it is hardly necessary to repudiate logic in order

19

to have aesthetic theory. We must rather examine these various theories in the light of the phenomena to be explained so that we can appraise the proposals each makes. Once we have examined them comparatively, it may then be possible to develop a comprehensive account of the data of aesthetics that retains the insights of previous attempts while avoiding their inadequacies. These shortcomings, as I shall attempt to show in this chapter, are of two somewhat related types. First, each theory commits the same methodological error in favoring certain of the data to be accounted for, yet offers itself as an exclusive and comprehensive explanation. But what is more crucial, each theory commits the identical logical error of equivocation by replacing the explanandum, that which is to be explained, with a surrogate that represents it inadequately. It is possible to avoid these difficulties by observing the methodological procedures and strictures already described. But we shall be better able to indicate the direction of a sound theory in aesthetics after examining critically some of the major theories that have already been proposed.

THE CRITICISM OF AESTHETIC THEORY

The criticism of theory in aesthetics, like the criticism of theory in any other field of inquiry, may follow any of several quite different directions. A theory may be judged (and most often is judged implicitly) according to the standards of the critic's own different position, and from that position found to be lacking. A clear example of this is the way in which formalists like Clive Bell and Roger Fry repudiate representational painting by insisting that the representational element in art is nonaesthetic. Yet they reject resemblance in favor of purely pictorial features like color, line, and composition on the basis of their own formalist theory. This same theory is the source of the sharp distinction they draw between emotions about life, evoked by the resemblance of forms to things outside art, and the aesthetic emotion that arises from the contemplation of the form itself. Imitation theory, however, which justifies the creation of representational art, claims that resemblance is of central aesthetic importance. Hence the criticism of imitation is made by means of an alien theory which consequently does not meet it on its own terms. The criticism of imitation from the position of a still different theory occurs when Eugene Véron derides the artist who is concerned with imitating as a person who is reducing himself to a copying machine. Yet this is a consequence of Véron's own emotionalist position, according to which the artist should attempt to express his individual feeling. Another illustration of this type of critical argument occurs when one denies that the artist's sincerity is aesthetically relevant on the grounds that to claim so is to commit the genetic fallacy. Yet, clearly, the defender of this position maintains it precisely because he is convinced, on grounds of his own theoretical standpoint, that not only is reference to the conditions of a work's creation pertinent, but that an account which ignores the artist's personality is by that fact erroneous. Still another case of this same critical approach consists in rejecting the possibility that contemporary drama can assume the dimensions of tragedy because there is no significant modern play which conforms to Aristotle's classic theory of tragedy. Here, again, a theory of tragedy which contemporary drama has deliberately not followed is used as the basis for judging it inferior to classical drama.

A related type of criticism is one made not from the standpoint of an alternative theory of aesthetics but rather from a commitment to a doctrine outside the domain of aesthetics entirely. Plato's atack on art from the standpoint of theory of knowledge is a famous illustration of this. For him, art can at best only imitate the appearance of things. Yet appearance, in its turn, is but a reflection of reality, and so art necessarily falsifies reality since it is thrice removed from it. Furthermore, the poet is also suspect. He claims to convey profound truths which he actually does not comprehend, because he writes not from knowledge but solely from inspiration. Moral grounds for criticizing art also figure significantly. Plato's criticism of Homer for describing the jealous, lascivious, and criminal behavior of the gods is a case in point. So, too, is Tolstoy's moralistic attack on art which does not communicate the religious perception of the times. Theories that derive their support from a particular religious allegiance often pursue a similar direction. They typically infer artistic strictures from the doctrines or policies of a religious movement or institution, and art that does not conform to them is censured. One illustration of this was the practice of Puritanism, which regarded art as frivolous and unworthy and therefore discouraged or dispensed with it entirely. Another case of the same kind of criticism was the promulgation of an official theory by the Council of Trent, by which the practice, and by implication the principles which guided such practice, of composers of ecclesiastical music and painters of religious subjects was to be regulated by theologians so as to subserve a strictly religious purpose.[1] A similar example is the judgment of art in the Soviet Union by an official secular theory of ideological origins. Here the politically based theory of socialist realism is used to attack artistic productions which fail to conform to the propagandistic uses they are expected to serve, on the grounds that they adhere to the bourgeois theory of "formalism." This mode of criticism is undoubtedly the one most frequently encountered, and we could multiply examples of it endlessly.

On the other hand, a position may be judged on the basis of difficulties that relate to its internal consistency or the adequacy of its concepts. This type of criticism is found less often than the previous one, but it has greater logical justification. Here a theory is regarded as an integral whole, and its concepts and principles analyzed in the light of their self-consistency and mutual compatibility. This manner of judging a theory occurs in the criticism of Suzanne Langer's proposal that a work of art is a presentational symbol, or C. J. Ducasse's view that art is an immediate symbol. These terms have been attacked for being self-contradictory, since symbols mediate between an object and a knower, and thus by their very nature cannot be immediate or direct. Another example of this type of criticism is the objections to the views of Véron and Tolstoy because of difficulties that arise from their emphasis on the artist's individuality or sincerity as the main factor in determining the value of

------

[1] *Vide Arnold Hauser, The Social History of Art,* Vol. 2 (New York, Vintage Books, n.d.), pp. 121 ff.

his work. In this case criticism does not deny the aesthetic relevance of individuality or sincerity; rather, it raises questions about whether we are able to determine if an artist has succeeded in expressing his personality or was sincere. To hold, as some writers have, that the only pertinent evidence of the artistic individuality or sincerity of a painter or writer lies exclusively in the work he has produced, virtually denies the usefulness of any reference to these traits at all. For if we are interested in the artistic sincerity or individuality of the creator, we are concerned not with the work but with the artist.

There is yet a third alternative for the criticism of theory, one that is found least frequently, perhaps, but that offers the greatest value. This type of criticism judges a proposal, neither on the basis of its internal consistency, nor by the external standard of a quite different position, but rather in the light of some independent objective basis common to all theories in a given field. This common basis is the body of data which a theory is devised to account for and which lies largely outside the conceptual framework of any theory. A successful theory formulates such data into factual statements and orders them into a comprehensive arrangement. In aesthetics, as we have seen, these data are the phenomena associated with the various facets of aesthetic experience, phenomena which form a relatively stable body of material and which can be formulated into different kinds of aesthetic facts. Here the arbitrariness of judgment is reduced to a minimum, since the independence of the data provides a firm support for common agreement. In this case, aesthetic theory is judged not only by its consistency and conceptual adequacy. It is judged as well by its ability to explain the relevant aesthetic facts, to account for new data, and to offer a satisfactory resolution of the problems that have constantly perplexed every aesthetic theory. One instance of this type of criticism is the objection voiced by Bernard Bosanquet and Joyce Cary to Croce's identification of artistic intuition with artistic expression on the grounds that this does not take into account the creative activity of the artist, who must work on his intuited idea and embody it in the materials of his craft. Only then can he fix and preserve its meaning. Yet this takes much effort and skill, and requires physical as well as imaginative effort, all of which Croce seems to ignore.

It is the last mode of criticism that I shall pursue here. Rather than throw up our hands in despair at the multitude of conflicting accounts of art, we need only return to a common base from which to begin our inquiry, and proceed from there to incorporate into a sounder framework the insights that have gone to compose seemingly irreconcilable theories.

I contend that the major attempts to explain art fail in being entirely satisfactory and convincing because they commit the same error of being false to the data of aesthetics. I shall illustrate this common failing by examining some of the explanations of art that are proposed most frequently, and then indicate how aesthetic theory might proceed in order to avoid such a difficulty. It is not my purpose here to offer a comprehensive account of each theory, hence the partial descriptions that follow ought not to be regarded as parodies of entire theories. In identifying and dealing with what I call surrogate theories of art, I am interested only in extrapolating in every instance a primary feature central to each of these theories, and in showing how in every case this feature functions as a surrogate for aesthetic experience, thus making inadequate the theory in which it is a leading element. While many of the specific objections are already familiar, they combine here to form a general critical judgment of significant force. This procedure should contribute both to clarifying aesthetic theory and to preparing the way for a proposal that aims to avoid this common defect.[2]

IMITATION THEORIES

Among the most obvious instances of surrogate theories are those which interpret art as an attempt to provide an accurate representation of the objects and events we experience. Art, according to the imitation theories, must be "realistic" and must depict its subject truly. The novel, the drama, the film, all

---

[2] Dewey embarks on a similar criticism of various theories of art that distort by seizing upon a particular aspect of experience in *Art as Experience* (1934), Ch. XII.

should be faithful mirrors of life and provide an accurate portrayal of human events. The improbable must be excluded. So, too, must the fine arts clearly represent their subjects. A painting must be a recognizable image and look like whatever it is portraying; a statue must resemble its model. Fidelity to the subject of the work is the keynote.

Mimesis may, of course, assume various forms. It may demand exactitude of representation, literal accuracy, as exemplified in Leonardo's insistence that "That painting is the most praiseworthy which is most like the thing represented." To this end, the artist may try to portray things as they really are by recording their exact proportions and details. Alternatively, he may attempt to imitate their appearance, and consequently employ devices like perspective and modeling which are designed to create an illusion of reality and which culminate in the techniques the impressionists developed to "imitate" the effects of light and atmosphere more successfully. Or, as during the neoclassical period, mimesis may be directed toward depicting universal properties, the essential nature or form of things. Here the artist is selective in what he represents, revealing the universal in the form of a particular. This version of imitation, unlike the preceding, can be applied to music, dance, and architecture. The imitation in dance may be of idealized action, or in music and architecture it may take on metaphysical overtones by imitating the form of beauty through balance and harmony. Again, as in the "theory of the affections" popular in Kant's day, music may be explained as imitating the diverse agitations of the soul.

Despite their apparent plausibility, however, mimetic theories no longer seem to offer a satisfactory account of art. In its more sophisticated versions, imitation goes beyond direct representation. By sanctioning illusion, it leads to the toleration of distortion, but in doing this it places in question the realistic thesis on which the theory rests. Moreover, the attempt to penetrate beneath the surface appearance of things directs imitation theories past perception into metaphysics, leaving outward resemblance far behind. Further still, a concern with the inward movement of a troubled soul ends by discarding any pretense of imitation in favor of more direct attention to emotion. And so, mimesis ends by transforming itself into an emotionalist theory.

This is not the place for a full discussion of the difficulties with imitation theories of art. Yet these theories suffer from a particular defect which follows from their very nature. By focusing the attention of both the creator and the perceiver beyond the work of art to the objects and events that are represented, mimesis interprets the activity of art as concerned with something outside the perceptual immediacy of the aesthetic situation. The extra-aesthetic obligations of the representational object force it beyond the experience of art, and that experience is itself understood and appraised by being related to something outside of and apart from itself, the thing being imitated. The point here is that the object being imitated acts as a surrogate for the inherently aesthetic character of the original experience. By leading the perceiver toward itself, away from the art work and outside the aesthetic situation, it substitutes a nonaesthetic object for the one that functions aesthetically.[3]

Furthermore, mimesis judges the artistic product by standards of accuracy or literal truth. By employing cognitive perception as their model, imitation theories apply the postanalytic standards of the knowledge process to the preanalytic experience of art. In this case, the cognitive object becomes a surrogate for the aesthetic object. Thus, in both respects, aesthetic perception is replaced by a nonaesthetic surrogate, either by the object or form represented, or by cognitive perception.[4]

---

[3] Edmund Burke reveals the final inadequacy of the imitation theory when he admits that an audience would empty a theater in which a most elaborate tragedy was about to be performed, if they heard that a state criminal of high rank was about to be hung nearby. Cf. *A Philosophical Enquiry* . . . (New York, 1958), p. 47.

The complete antithesis of this occurs in Sartre's suggestive observation that "Sculpture suggests movement, painting depth or light. Calder suggests nothing; he captures and embellishes true, living movements. His mobiles signify nothing, refer to nothing other than themselves; they simply are, they are absolutes." *Essays in Aesthetics* (New York, Philosophical Library, 1963), p. 79.

[4] My second argument here rests on the supposition that aesthetic perception is preanalytic and therefore radically different from the cognitive process. The view that art is noncognitive is a central thesis of this book, and it will be discussed in some detail in Chapter IV. Here it is only necessary to acknowledge that art is different from the literal knowledge-gathering activity of the sciences. This is a much milder form of the thesis, and is rarely disputed today.

EMOTIONALIST THEORIES

Seeking and being guided by feeling in attending to art continues to be a motive that is popular among artists and audiences alike. In particular, the affective force of art objects is taken as the standard by which they are judged. While emotionalist theories are widely held and occur in a variety of forms, they commit an error which resembles that of the imitation theories. They do so less in their own right, however, than in the ways in which they are interpreted and developed.

It would be hard to dispute seriously the fact that an emotional component can be discerned in the experience of art. It can be found in the experience of almost anything. Moreover, in giving major importance to the experiential factor in aesthetics, emotionalist theories of art constitute a significant advance beyond the imitation theories. Yet this is soon overshadowed by the way in which the emotional aspect of aesthetic experience is typically described and interpreted. It is lame and perhaps futile to speak of the emotional component of experience by using general terms like "joyful," "sorrowful," "exhilarating," "depressing," and "exciting." Any one of these epithets might be applied with equal ease to an indefinite number of otherwise remarkably dissimilar art works, and it helps very little to resort to strings of such descriptive terms. Furthermore, the vocabulary in which we talk about emotions is impoverished in contrast with the richness of emotional experience. In ascribing a single such term or even a combination of them to an art object, one succeeds more in misrepresenting and distorting than in characterizing it. How insipid is the description of a musical composition as sad, tragic, amusing or cheerful! Moreover, if we select a single type of emotional reaction like pleasure, we merely seize upon a common kind of affective experience and generalize it to cover all cases of aesthetic response. Besides being uninformative, reference to pleasure unduly limits the variety and scope of aesthetic experience by confining it to a single facet of its emotional quality. We are likewise unable to overcome the difficulty by referring to a peculiarly aesthetic emotion which is aroused by the significant formal relations of the work. To describe aesthetic experience as one in which an "aesthetic emotion" is present begs the question of its identifiable feature. It assumes that such experience is emotional in quality and yet tells us nothing positive about it. It simply isolates a peculiarly aesthetic quality of the experience from other emotional tones of human experience and maintains that it is entirely unlike the emotions of "life," while telling us nothing about what makes it different. It is hard to see where this differs from mere stipulation.

At most, the explanation of art by means of one or several emotions provides but a partial account. The emotional element is just one of the factors that we are able to discern when we reflect on the experience of art. Other features may be present, such as interest, recognition of motifs, forms or ideas, acute perceptual awareness, intuitive insight, perception of relationships, and the like. Moreover, during the experience and before reflecting on it, the emotional component is fused with all the other aspects of experience. To characterize the totality of an experience by its emotional component is at best to indulge in synecdoche by mistaking a part of aesthetic experience for the whole experience; to do so at worst aborts it. In either case, emotion becomes a surrogate for full aesthetic experience.

Perhaps only by using a term with great inclusiveness, as when Suzanne Langer employs "feeling" to mean "everything that can be felt, from physical sensation, pain and comfort, excitement and response, to the most complex emotions, intellectual tensions, or the steady feeling-tones of a conscious human life,"[5] can one hope to avoid falsification. Such generality, however, makes feeling equivalent to the entire range of human experience of which we may become aware, and goes well beyond emotionalism. Furthermore, a notion as broad as this does little to help us account for the emotional quality of specific art works, nor does it yet explain the way in which feeling is manifested or the significance of art in human emotional experience. We are thus led to those theories which interpret art as expressing, communicating, or symbolizing emotion.

_____

[5] *Problems of Art* (New York, 1957), p. 15.

EXPRESSION THEORIES

One of the most common ways of accounting for art in current discussions is to explain it as a mode of expression. We often speak of a painting or a symphonic movement as being expressive, or we ask what the author, painter, or composer is trying to express in a work. Indeed, we sometimes wonder what the work itself expresses.

Because of their popularity, the expression theories have received extensive discussion. While this is not the place for a thoroughgoing critique of the various forms of expression theory, it is important to raise certain objections to any attempt to characterize art as expressive. In whatever way they are formulated, theories of art as expression entail one or another kind of misrepresentation. Art has been interpreted by expression theories as expressing different kinds of things. Some writers cite emotion, others ideas, and still others cite images as the things being expressed. Each of these proposals, however, presents certain difficulties.

It is perhaps most frequent for expression theories to speak about the expression of emotion. Yet such a theory of art misdirects our attention. This version of expression explains art, neither by the art object nor by the full experience of art, but by going beyond both either to the emotion being expressed (in which case the criticisms of emotionalist theories apply) or to its source in the artist's impulses, motives, and needs. Either alternative, though, leaves us with a surrogate theory. The first does this by reducing the fullness of aesthetic experience to an abstracted emotional component, and the second by taking us outside art to the biography of the artist.

Sometimes it is argued, however, that art expresses ideas rather than emotions. Still, to say that art expresses ideas directs our attention away from the perceptual qualities of the aesthetic object and our direct encounter with it, and focuses instead on the belief being expressed. This shifts our interest from the features which make our experience of art intrinsically and uniquely interesting, and occupies us with matters quite independent of any aesthetic concern. Did Brutus really betray Caesar, as Shakespeare suggests? Was the massacre on the third day of May, 1808, an actual event, and was it as savage and unjust as Goya's painting depicts? Were the conditions of human life as stark, exploitative, and dehumanizing as realistic painters like Millet and naturalistic novelists like Frank Norris, Dreiser, Zola, and others described them? Here cognitive standards of truth are relevant, and our concern is not with art as art, but with the sifting of evidence and the validity of inference, so as to arrive at an accurate belief. Again a surrogate for art enters in the form of ideational meaning and truth, and we are led away from aesthetic responsiveness to matters of historical and social fact.

To say, finally, that rather than expressing emotion or ideas, art expresses images in any literal sense, leads us to interpret art through its effect on the imagination. This tends to take us away from the art object and beyond aesthetic perception to the images the art work excites. Now it is undeniable that imaginative processes play a necessarily large role in the experience of certain arts. Literature, in particular, relies heavily on an imaginative response. Yet it is equally undeniable that the images stimulated, especially in connection with other arts, are frequently irrelevant to the art work that acts as stimulus. Music and painting are all too often used merely to set in motion a train of daydreams or fantasies which have no connection with the art objects that excite them. Their imaginative appeal here revives difficulties that are similar to those from which imitation theories suffered. By directing our attention away from experience that centers on the art object, the images act as surrogates for aesthetic perception.

There are, in addition, some general difficulties which all versions of the expression theory entail. To regard art as expression focuses on only one part of the situation in which art occurs. It calls attention first to the art object in an attempt to understand its expressive qualities. Yet by its interest in the expressiveness of the object, this theory moves quite naturally to the source of these qualities, and thus tends to lead us still farther away from the situation, by making us concerned less with the object itself than with its genesis and the artist who created it. Here expression becomes the combined result of what the artist intended and of how he produced his work. But in doing this, the expression theory incurs in some measure the intentional fallacy, and more generally, the genetic fallacy. By directing our attention to the origin of the art object and to the artist's expressive motives, a surrogate replaces the functioning of the art object in the aesthetic situation. Etienne Gilson put the point well when he observed that "What makes self-expression beautiful is not that it is expression, but rather that, taken in itself, it is a thing of beauty enjoyable for its own sake."[6]

Yet the concern of aesthetics is properly with art rather than biography. The farther we remove ourselves from the art object and the situation in which it functions, the more distant we become from any strictly aesthetic interest. Even by returning to the object of art so that we may examine it for its expressive clues, the difficulties with this theory remain. For we may well ask, how can art *express* anything? Without going into semantic details, are we not speaking metaphorically here of aesthetic experience? Is not calling an object expressive simply a way of testifying to the effectiveness with which the work functions in our experience? Clearly, to speak of an *object* as being expressive or as expressing something is to interpret it animistically. The *objec*t is neither expressive nor is *it* expressing anything; it is *we* who regard it as having significance. The object itself simply is. And so expression theories oblige us to return to the experience of art.

COMMUNICATION THEORIES

We do not overcome these difficulties by interpreting art as communication rather than as expression. Communication theories cover a wide variety of positions, from Croce's subsumption of art as an intuitive expressive activity under the general theory of linguistic, to the popular description of music as "the language of the emotions." All such attempts to explain art do see it as a species of human activity, yet they fail to supply a satisfactory explanation of its distinctive features. They assume that art performs the same kind of function that language

---

[6] *The Arts of the Beautiful* (New York, Scribners, 1965), p. 61.

does, and by interpreting the aesthetic activity as a communicative one, the experience of art is again replaced by a surrogate.

Language is a device for embodying and communicating meaning through the use of symbols. Except for special occasions, language is rarely reflexive. Its value is preeminently instrumental. Intrinsically, language is relatively unimportant, and we seldom concentrate our attention on it except when we use it as an artistic medium or as the subject matter of linguistic science or philosophy. How different is this from a description of the function of art. Whereas language points beyond itself, the art object plays a key role in aesthetic experience and becomes the focal point of intrinsic perceptual awareness. Indeed, the explanation of art on an analogy with language is one of the most widespread and one of the most mendacious theories. It distracts us from the qualities of the aesthetic situation and leads us to expect from art what it is least able to supply.

Those theories which seize on the surface resemblance of art to linguistic activity invariably attribute meaning to art. Yet again, in any *literal* sense, this is foreign to aesthetic experience. To say that a painting or a sonata has meaning refers at most, not to the work itself, but to the perceiver's experience of profundity or to the associations or reverberations it creates in his memory. It is his experience projected as an attribute of the art work. To speak of meaning is to refer literally to a cognitive feature; any other sense is metaphorical. Yet if anyone should seek information from a poem, we would not regard him as exhibiting an aesthetic interest or response. Indeed, we generally regard cognitive meaning as being embodied in statements or propositions, and these are independent of specific languages with their peculiar traits. But in art it is the individual, unique characteristics which are indispensable. Whatever meaning an art work may be said to have is inseparable from these features. As A. C. Bradley expressed so well, the poet "meant what he said, and said what he meant. . . . Meaning they [a Beethoven symphony or a Turner picture] have, but *what* meaning can be said in no language but their own."[7] Any

---

[7] "Poetry for Poetry's Sake," reprinted in Rader, *op. cit.*, p. 321.

change in the work changes its meaning. In fact, Bradley denies that art has meaning in its literal, cognitive sense at all. Moreover, those attempts to rescue the notion of meaning by taking it in an emotive rather than a cognitive sense are also unsatisfactory. Besides encountering the difficulties of the emotionalist theories, the reference to emotive "meaning" is at best metaphorical. It reveals the pervasive presence of an intellectualist bias which insists that emotion be construed in cognitive terms.

By attributing meaning to art, we are, at most, calling attention to its importance, to the significance of the experience of art. But reference to meaning in art, like reference to language, tends to be misleading and ends by replacing art with a surrogate. Art, however, must be taken on its own terms. Archibald MacLeish's "Ars Poetica" captures this insight, especially in its famous lines, "A poem should not mean / But be."[8] It is what it is as it is; no more, no less.

Symbolic theories of art offer perhaps the most salient examples of surrogate theories. While employed with considerable ingenuity and insight by Cassirer, Panofsky, Langer and others, art, when interpreted as symbolic form, becomes the emissary of meaning. Here again art leaves the aesthetic and enters the realm of the cognitive.[9] This is equally true of all such theories, whether art be taken as the symbol of the artist and his times, as a religious symbol, as an emotional symbol, as a psychoanalytic symbol, or as a poetic archetype.

It is curious to observe the various ways in which the need to attribute meaning to art results in the *ad hoc* attachment of symbolic significance to it. I. A. Richards, even while recogniz-

---

[8] *Collected Poems*, p. 41.

[9] This is clearly illustrated in Panofsky's analysis of meaning in painting into four layers: recognizable objects and events (recognition involves an associative process of cognition, relating past learning to present experience), the style of a period (distinguishing style requires a body of scholarship which must be employed in the cognitive process of analyzing a work), allegorical figures or types (awareness of universal types requires the use of abstractive techniques), and finally the intrinsic, philosophical significance which embodies its symbolic function (this involves fitting art into the schema of a philosophic system). Cf. *Studies in Iconology* (New York, Oxford University Press, 1939), p. 16. According to the criticisms developed in this chapter, the significance of painting on each of these levels lies outside the object and the experience in which it participates.

ing the prior importance of the sensory aspect of most poetry, interprets poetry mainly as the evocative use of signs, particularly by means of metaphors.[10] Langer's suggestion is perhaps more tenable when she describes art as an extended metaphor or nondiscursive symbol that expresses what language cannot express—the immediacy of experience.[11] And yet the closer Langer comes to relating art to the direct perception of experience, the less art functions as a symbol and the more it asserts itself in its own right. The commitment to a communication theory combines with the awareness of the direct immediacy of aesthetic experience to lead her ironically to the self-contradictory notion of art as a presentational symbol. And even Ducasse, who gives prominence to the directness of the aesthetic response, is drawn into the same odd posture when he interprets the aesthetic object as the "immediate symbol" of an emotion, so embodying it that we receive the "taste" of that emotion by directly apprehending the symbol.[12]

Theories of art which employ the notion of a symbol, as in those developed by Langer and Ducasse, distort the usual meaning of symbol. They appear more concerned to retain the common association of art with meaning that so typifies aesthetic intellectualism, than to rest on the experience they are supposed to explain.[13]

---

[10] "Many, if not most, of the statements in poetry are there *as means* to the manipulation and expression of feelings and attitudes. . . ." *Practical Criticism* (New York, Harcourt, Brace, 1929), p. 186.

[11] *Problems of Art*, pp. 24-26.

[12] *Art, the Critics, and You* (New York, 1944), p. 179.

[13] For a general criticism of such semiotic theories, especially that of Charles W. Morris, see Richard Rudner, "On Semiotic Aesthetics," *Journal of Aesthetics and Art Criticism*, 10 (1951), pp. 67-77. Rudner also gives a good defense of non-semiotic aesthetics, particularly against theories of expression, in "Some Problems of Non-Semiotic Aesthetic Theories," same journal, 15, pp. 298-310. The statements of artists (and their expositors) contain many attempts to express the directness of aesthetic experience, although they are often couched in the terminology of conventional theoretical accounts. Henry Moore, for example, has written, "For me a work must first have a vitality *of its own*. I do *not* mean *a reflection* of the vitality of life, of movement, physical action, frisking, dancing figures and so on, but that a work can have in it a pent-up energy, an intense life of its own, independent of the object it may represent. When work has this powerful vitality we do not connect the word beauty with it." (Italics mine.) And Herbert Read, developing Moore's point, explains,

Yet there is a directness to the experience of art which the more perceptive symbolic theories feel compelled to acknowledge, and it is this immediacy which is incompatible with describing art as language or symbol. The linguistic theory of Croce reflects the identical influence, for he makes much of the intuitive individuality of aesthetic forms and emphasizes the untranslatability of aesthetic expressions.[14]

What Langer and Ducasse seem to be saying in a circuitous way is not that art functions as a symbol ordinarily does, but rather that the art object is not complete and self-sufficient. Instead it must be regarded as a factor in the larger context of experience. This observation is both correct and important, but it is misrepresented by a theory that by its literal content removes the art object from the involvement it properly has in aesthetic experience. At best these descriptions are merely suggestive metaphors. Yet there is no place in theory for metaphors. A theoretical account should properly provide a literal explanation. As a whole, then, the communication theories are surrogate theories. They commit the error of confusing the reflective analytic, symbol-using attitude and activity with the inherently noncognitive aesthetic ones.

FORMALIST THEORIES

It can readily be shown how all the major theories of art embroil themselves in difficulties similar to those just described. It is not necessary, however, to provide an exhaustive account of every theory to establish the point of this criticism. Let me conclude, then, with a final example of a surrogate theory, a

---

[14] Benedetto Croce, *Aesthetic* (New York, 1958), pp. 67-68.

"The terms of the debate [between beauty and vitality] need careful definition, but obviously the whole scope of art is altered if you make it, instead of the more or less sensuous symbolization of intellectual ideals, *the direct expression of an organic vitalism*. No doubt intellectual elements will enter into the choice and elaboration of the images which the intellect selects to represent its ideals, but the difference is about as wide as is humanly possible." (Italics mine.) (From Henry Moore, "The Sculptor's Aims," in Herbert Read, ed., *Unit One*, 1934, p. 30; and Herbert Read, *The Philosophy of Modern Art* (New York, 1952), p. 207. Both are reprinted in M. Weitz, ed., *Problems in Aesthetics* (New York, 1959), pp. 511 and 513.

theory to which it might seem difficult to object because this theory, more than any discussed so far, endeavors to explain art on its own peculiar terms, and thus arrive at a more authentic statement than earlier theories of what art is about.

Formalism came as a revolutionary corrective to a history of misleading and unquestioned assumptions about art. Never before had the representative character of the graphic and plastic arts been so challenged, at least in theory. Yet Roger Fry, Clive Bell, and others insisted on the startling position that the representational element in art was nonaesthetic and, indeed, that it distracted the perceiver from the genuinely pictorial qualities such as line, color, mass, and plane that he ought properly to be concerned with. Several decades earlier, Eduard Hanslick had championed absolute music against music with programmatic content. He insisted that the listener occupy himself exclusively with musical elements like sound and motion, and not use music as an emotional stimulus. Most recently, the New Criticism in literature also bears an affinity to the same general position, in its emphasis on the literary use of language with its levels of meaning, its associations, rhythms and formal arrangements. Despite the importance of its insights, though, formalism establishes both too much and too little.

Formalism developed as an attack on the imitation theory which was widely used to condemn modern nonrepresentational art. In rejecting the aesthetic relevance of representation, however, formalism construed it exclusively in terms of a theory of simple imitation. Yet it is possible to retain the recognizable image as a legitimate part of the painting itself, and to regard its significance as determined entirely by its place in the painting. Instead of representation or resemblance, which imply reference to something outside the painting that is reproduced in it, we can speak rather of presentation or semblance, in which the image is viewed in its own right and not primarily as a sign of something else. Certainly one can regard recognizable images as doing more than recording appearances or reminding one of outside associations. Within the painting the image is something quite different from what it would be when taken only as a reminder. It may function to inform and enhance the total perceptual effect, by introducing ideas, associations, and feelings that are transformed through being embodied in an art object. These then add to and benefit from the peculiarly painterly qualities of the medium.

Hence formalism excludes from the data of aesthetics much that need not be cast out on aesthetic grounds. It is certainly not true that all art must be representational. Yet the converse of this, that representational painting may be art, is not likewise false. Representational art may be aesthetic by virtue of its representational features, and the range of objects we regard aesthetically includes both the representational and the non-representational. Formalism thus establishes more than it need. It is enough to justify abstract art without excluding the representational in the process. One difficulty with formalism, then, is that the nonrepresentational form becomes a surrogate for the whole range of aesthetically perceivable images.

Formalism also errs in proving too little. In their anxiety to restrict attention to purely artistic elements, the formalists seem inclined to focus almost entirely on the art object. Their attention is wrapped up in the pictorial qualities of the painting, the literary features of the poem or novel, or the structural components of the musical composition. Certainly this is an improvement over a theory such as emotionalism, in which the art object is apt to be forgotten in the concern with the feelings of the person appreciating it.

To insist that we confine our aesthetic attention to the painting, poem, or musical work, *per se,* is to limit us unduly, however. For them to be the center of the perceiver's attention does not mean that other factors may not play an important role in our appreciation of art. There are connections with experience beyond the perception of form alone that may be aesthetically relevant. The art object does not exist in a world by itself; it rather occupies a place in the broad matrix of human experience. Art's indictment of social evils, its commentary on human relationships, its championing of new ideas and causes all suggest connections more inclusive and profound than the formalists are willing to admit. Theirs is an inverted romanticism that would keep out the philistine figures of culture, history, and technology from the sacred grove of art.

It might seem that Bell and Fry have corrected any over-emphasis on the painting by introducing a peculiarly "aesthetic emotion" in the perceiver to indicate that a painting possesses "significant form." Unfortunately this lays their position open to the criticisms of emotionalism that we have already detailed. For this singular and rare emotion fragments the experience of art, cutting it off from the breadth which that experience can assume. It restricts aesthetic experience in a manner precisely parallel to the way in which it would confine our aesthetic perception to the formal elements in a work of art. We must conclude, then, that in this respect, too, formalism is a surrogate theory. It replaces the full scope of the social origins, experience, and relevance of art with a sacrosanct object, protected by the hallowed walls of the museum and nurtured in the sensitive soul of the esthete.

CONTRIBUTIONS OF THE SURROGATE THEORIES

Despite the force of these criticisms it is not my contention that all the theories examined here are entirely false. Indeed I am ready to recognize their individual merits, for we cannot dismiss summarily theories that have been taken as seriously as these by so many perceptive minds. Each, in fact, contains a true and important insight, yet because this observation is part of a surrogate theory, it is obscured and often misinterpreted. Let me suggest then, at this point, where the contribution of each of these theories lies.

In the case of imitation theories, it is not nature, appearance, or reality which must be slavishly emulated. Art, nonetheless, must be "true to life" in that it must bring us into direct contact with the immediacy of our experience. Art is not the occasion for an isolated esoteric mode of response, open only to the initiate and unconnected with anything else. The encounter with art is more than a magical escape from life; it is more than a peculiar sort of occurrence, independent of the rest of human interests. On the contrary, successful art evokes a response from the reservoir of man's readiness to react to the events in which he is involved. Art, indeed, has a deep and important connection with the life of man, yet obviously this varies with the particular art and with the style or movement. Nineteenth century realism in literature, for example, emphasizes the closeness of this relationship, and Georg Lukacs made a perceptive observation when he noted that "Great literature . . . reveals a 'piece of life' providing more truthful and more profound reflection of reality than is generally obtained in ordinary life." Clearly the same holds true for those arts that embody social criticism. Pop art, to take a recent example, rests largely on its connections with the experiences of popular culture. It can best be understood, not for its formal qualities, but for the implied social commentary of its subject matter. In this respect it succeeds admirably in forcing us to see the oppressive vulgarity of our commercial culture. It is even true that the sensory awareness of the most stylized and abstract art objects carries associations for us, and the most ardent defenders of modern nonrepresentational art have acknowledged this. Ortega y Gasset admits this when he observes that "Perhaps in the most abstract ornamental line there vibrates as in disguise a tenacious reminiscence of certain 'natural' forms." And Roger Fry, after vehemently attacking representational painting and arguing for the aesthetic relevance of only formal qualities, comes in intellectual honesty to admit a tenuous connection of art with the emotions of life.[15] There would seem, then, to be an intimate connection that art has, not necessarily with the appearances of things, but rather with our *experiences* of them. Art can intensify the rest of human experience, and this experience can, in turn, enhance the significance of art. It is the whole man that experiences art, and art influences the whole man.

The insights of the other theories we have considered are

---

[15] "Now, from our definition of this pure beauty, the emotional tone is not due to any recognizable reminiscence or suggestion of the emotional experiences of life; but I sometimes wonder if it nevertheless does not get its force from arousing some very deep, very vague, and immensely generalized reminiscences. It looks as though art had got access to the substratum of all the emotional colors of life; to something which underlies all the particular and specialized emotions of actual life. It seems to derive an emotional energy from the very conditions of our existence by its relation of an emotional significance in time and space. Or it may be that art really calls up, as it were, the residual traces left on the spirit by the different emotions of life, without however recalling the actual experiences, so that we get an echo of the emotion without the limitation and particular direction which it had in experience." Roger Fry, *The Hogarth Essays*, 1924, "The Artist and Psychoanalysis."

more obvious. By involving the personal human response as an essential component of the aesthetic situation, the emotionalist theories have provided a contribution of signal importance in the understanding of art. Art can hardly be understood with any accuracy apart from the way it functions in human experience, and the emotional element in experience is an undeniable one. The emotionalist theories, then, rightly move us away from any position that would elevate and eternalize art objects by removing them from their dependency on experience. They return art squarely to its human setting. Also, the theories of art as expression and communication make us aware of the fact that art involves much more than subjective experience. Art is a social event. It possesses social significance through the community of human experience. This is an essential factor in the understanding of art, one which no comprehensive theory can afford to overlook. Finally, the formalist theories rightly emphasize the central role that the art object plays in aesthetic experience. The object, rather than the artist, the observer, or the subject-matter, is the proper focus of our perceptual attention.

There is, then, significant merit in each of these theories. In every case, however, the insight is obscured by the surrogate character of the theory that is developed. What a full account of art must do is retain these insights while avoiding their distortions.

BEYOND SURROGATE THEORIES

It is possible to discover in the history of aesthetic theory a growing tendency to handle the phenomena of art as the subject of an autonomous inquiry. The historical sequence of theories that have been proposed is not a coincidental sequence but rather a developmental one. It seems to reflect the cumulative development of our understanding of aesthetic perception. The earlier theories like mimesis tended to confuse the aesthetic function with recording appearances and historical events, and with preserving and communicating information.[16] This con-

---

[16] This is aptly illustrated by the observation in Samuel Johnson's *Preface to Shakespeare* that "The end of writing is to instruct; the end of poetry is to instruct by pleasing."

tinued even when the imitation was ideal rather than real, for
art then served the purpose of leading men to the apprehension
of a higher, spiritual order of being and impressing upon them a
moral ideal. The rise of emotionalist theories signified that art
was more important than before, that it was doing something
nothing else could do. These theories recognized the place of
originality and creativity. They discovered the personal element
in artistic perception and the intrinsic importance of the experience of art. For the first time, art was seen as something valuable
in its own right which had to be regarded disinterestedly. By
stressing the role of the creative artist and of the personal
response to art, the emotionalist theories led to the emancipation
of the artist and perceiver from the manifestly nonaesthetic
concerns of the imitation theories. Yet emotionalism swung
theory too much in the opposite direction, so that it became
excessively concerned with matters of personality, motives,
biography, and other questions of psychological and historical
interest. Thus the advent of formalism served as a corrective
by directing our attention back to the aesthetic features of the
art object. Whereas emotionalism led to the emancipation of
the artist, formalism achieved the emancipation of the art object
and its medium. Now the object had become independent and
had to be regarded for its purely aesthetic qualities.

Certainly this succession of theories does not present a set
of logically exclusive alternatives for the explanation of art. I
have already noted in the preceding section how each can be
seen to contribute its own peculiar insight to what art is about.
Yet the sequence of theories reveals a highly significant trend
toward interpreting art on its own terms, toward freeing it from
subordinance to religious, moral, cognitive, and political influences, and this has considerable significance. Moreover, while
many of these theories have been losing their hold somewhat,
the emancipation of aesthetic theory is still far from complete.
The way in which art is approached, the fashion in which it is
described, and the manner in which it is interpreted all testify,
as I have tried to show, to the incompleteness of its liberation.

Undoubtedly, one of the greatest difficulties in interpreting
the nature of art results from the need to give a clear description

of a mode of experience that differs in certain key respects from every other. It is this difficulty which leads the most widely held theories to account for art, not on the basis of our experience of its own traits, but by relating or identifying it with other kinds of things that are more clearly understood and more easily designated. Just as animistic explanations of physical events were used before the advent of modern science to account for the new and strange by interpreting them in the manner of human actions which were more familiar, the phenomena of aesthetics have thus far been described in the commonly recognized but nonaesthetic terms of imitation, emotion, language, and the like. Surrogate theories, however, do an injustice to art by reducing aesthetic experience to nonperceptual, literally nonaesthetic modes of experience, or to stereotyped and limited kinds of experience. Perhaps because these theories are discursive attempts to formulate the inherently nondiscursive experience of art, they fail to take proper account of the peculiar features of aesthetic experience, translating it instead into other, more readily identifiable kinds.

Of course one may object that every theory is an attempt to codify experience into recognizable types. Why, then, should aesthetic theory be castigated merely for doing the same? The objection lies not with aesthetic theorizing *per se,* but with the failure to apprehend the characteristic traits of aesthetic experience by reducing it to alien modes. While an account of aesthetic experience is the task of the next chapter, the previous one has already made sufficiently clear the case for a distinguishable kind of perceptual experience associated with art. And if only we grant that aesthetic experience has an identity of its own, the force of the criticisms presented here is undeniable. A mode of experience distinguishable from other kinds can hardly be adequately represented by them.[17] That is why attempts to

---

[17] I emphatically disclaim any intention of subscribing to what I. A. Richards has termed "the phantom aesthetic state." (cf. his *Principles of Literary Criticism,* ch. 2). In arguing for the identity of an aesthetic mode of experience, I do not hold that it is a rarified condition discontinuous with any other. Quite the contrary; I am convinced that the experience associated with art and aesthetic value shares many features in common with other kinds of experience, and that it is not only continuous with but pervasive in the perceptual activities of men.

interpret art as feeling, as emotion, as pleasure or as form do injury to the richness and inclusiveness of aesthetic experience when they merely abstract a commonly recognized facet of experience and ascribe it to art. And that is why theories that interpert art as mimesis, as a means of expression, as a language for communication, or as a symbol are misrepresentations, for these all interpret the experience of art as ultimately referential, as being like or about something other than itself.

TOWARD A THEORY OF AESTHETIC EXPERIENCE

I am certainly not suggesting that all efforts to theorize about aesthetics are cursed. Nor am I implying that, since aesthetic experience is preanalytic, it cannot be inquired into. My critic-isms are directed rather to the failure of aesthetics to treat aesthetic experience in the light of its own distinctive character-istics. I am proposing, instead, that aesthetic theory become genuinely empirical, that it be guided not by prior commitments or preconceptions from outside aesthetic experience but by the intrinsic qualities of such experience, and that it study man's experiences of art in their characteristic setting. One important consequence of this approach to theorizing is that we must reject those interpretations that displace the distinctive experiences of art by reducing them to a mode of experience different from the aesthetic. We must put aside explanations with animistic and biographical overtones, like expression and communication theories. Finally, we must dispense with all surrogates for aesthetic experience. While these may have some explanatory value, they are solely metonymical and ought to be replaced by a literal account. Speaking analogically, what is needed is a reformation in aesthetic theory that would be achieved by supplanting the priesthood of the surrogate theories by the protestantism of direct communion with experience that art is able to furnish.

We have not sufficiently realized that aesthetic theory is,

Indeed, when we direct our attention primarily to the experience rather than the object and materials of the arts, we are led to discover the continuity of the aesthetic mode with other kinds of experience, and to recognize the ubiquity of aesthetic perception in human life.

literally speaking, metaaesthetics. If we acknowledged the major importance of the perceptual aspect of aesthetic experience (as it is suggested in the etymology of the term "aesthetics"— *aisthēsis,* sense perception), we should come to realize that aesthetic theory is talk about a kind of experience which such talk itself is not. Yet this condition is not peculiar to aesthetics. It is the case with the natural and behavioral sciences too. Only in linguistics, semantics, the philosophy of logic, methodology, and theory construction is this not so. Perhaps the problem here arises out of the attempt to render in concepts what is actually a recognizable type of experience that is itself of quite a different order. Indeed, as I shall suggest, a large share of the difficulty lies in the fact that aesthetic experience is non-conceptual, and the discursive nature of language is foreign to the nondiscursive nature of art. Thus the failure to distinguish clearly between aesthetic experience and the theory of aesthetic experience has led recently to scepticism in some quarters about the very possibility of aesthetics, since it seems impossible to get at the nature of art without ending up with a closed definition that cannot do justice to the limitless variety of the experience of art. And it is not difficult to understand also why the artist, by his precognitive reliance on the totality of perceptual awareness, is drawn often to express his experiences in the evocative language of the metaphysician or the mystic.

The conclusion to which we are drawn regarding the ways in which art has been theorized about is that the study of aesthetics has not proceeded beyond a preliminary stage. Aesthetic theory still, for the most part, looks outside the experience of art to explain art. Most theories replace aesthetic experience with a surrogate, and while this may serve to dispel puzzlement, it is at the expense of accuracy. Yet it is the task of theory in aesthetics to provide a literal rather than a metaphorical account of aesthetic experience. For a metaphorical theory is a surrogate theory, and aesthetic theory with pretensions to truthfulness must forego metaphor and deal with the experience and phenomena of art in their own terms.

My purpose here has been to point up the need to develop a rigorous descriptive science of aesthetics based on a deliberate and careful examination of aesthetic experience on its own terms. To render aesthetics scientific does not mean that the distinctive characteristics and special values of aesthetic experience must be discounted or lost. For it is the *theory* of art which must develop into an empirical science and not art, itself, or the experience it evokes. What this does mean, however, is rather that there is the opportunity here to achieve a fuller awareness of the conditions under which aesthetic experience may take place, of the significance of such experiences for human life, and of the role of art in human culture. But in pursuing the goal of an empirical aesthetics, we must observe the dictum, adapt the theory to art, not art to the theory. Only then will we be able to enhance the totality of human experience by truly recognizing its aesthetic dimension.

III

THE AESTHETIC FIELD

AFTER THESE FAR-REACHING criticisms of past aesthetic theory, we face the problem of developing a theory that will embody the insights of traditional aesthetics, while avoiding its mischaracterizations. It is easier, indeed, to point out difficulties than to overcome them. Furthermore, it is not enough to be content with describing aesthetic experience negatively by stating that art is not primarily cognitive, expressive, imitative, symbolic, or communicative in order to avoid the problems of these common proposals. Like negative theology, a negative aesthetics can succeed at most in avoiding error, never in illuminating. It is only by providing a positive account of art that aesthetic theory can be reestablished on a new and sounder foundation. Now that the case against surrogate theories has been made, let us explore the direction a valid aesthetics must take.

THE CONCEPT OF THE AESTHETIC FIELD

It is a strange fact in the history of aesthetics that explanations of art have nearly always had structural limitations. Not only have surrogates distorted the various accounts; the referents of the different theories have also been one-sided and fragmentary.

A glance at some representative theories will bear this out. Imitation focuses on nature and life, and only secondarily on the art object. When *mimesis* speaks of the object, it does so merely to compare it with the real or ideal subject matter the object is supposed to reflect. The formalists, on the contrary, direct their attention almost entirely to the art object alone. Their aesthetic interest lies solely in the way in which the medium of paint, sound, or language is used. So, too, do the

46

emotionalists of various sorts confine themselves largely to a single aspect of art. For them, only the feelings of the artist and the perceiver are relevant, and the object is reduced largely to the role of promoting these. Such approaches to art all seize on one aspect of the activity and thereby do an injustice to the others. And on those occasions when reference is made to both the perceiver and the art object, one or the other of them still dominates the account, and the distinction between them is generally ill-drawn and inconsistently executed.[1]

The same limitation is reflected in the various meanings given the term 'art.' Most often, perhaps, 'art' refers to the class of art objects—paintings, novels, poems, statues, musical compositions, and the like. It is in this sense that the formalists use the term. Sometimes, though, its denotation shifts. 'Art' may be used in its etymological sense to signify the creative activity. 'Art' here is the process of making artistic objects and participating in artistic events. Again, 'art' may connote aesthetic value; to call something 'art' is to praise it as aesthetically good. Yet another sense of the term is its use to denote aesthetic experience, however that may be described. 'Art' is experiencing things aesthetically, either as intuitive expression with Croce, as intrinsic perception with Gotshalk, as an integral experience with Dewey, or as pleasure with Ducasse.

To speak of 'art' in any of these senses, however, is to utter a partial truth. For art is all these and more. It can, in fact, only be defined by making reference to the total situation in which the objects, activities, and experiences of art occur, a setting which includes all these denotata and more. This I shall call the *aesthetic field*, the context in which art objects are actively and creatively experienced as valuable. It is this inclusive setting which we must examine in its entirety before we can give an accurate explanation of what art is and answer the questions which continue to plague aesthetic theory. Anything less than this cannot help but embody the distortions of a fragmentary account.

------

[1] "The history of aesthetics is, in a word, essentially a history of explanations of different fields or different phases of the arts." V. Tejera, *Art and Human Intelligence* (New York, Appleton-Century-Crofts, 1965), p. 17.

Whatever else art may be, it is human experience. In this respect it is no different from anything else in man's universe. Yet while all the individual features that are found in aesthetic experience appear in every mode of experience, the aesthetic mode possesses its own identity. We can say, for instance, that art is perceptual experience by a biosocial creature that occurs in time. Yet this can be said of experiences that are not primarily aesthetic, and we must still explain the specific part that each of these features plays when we are aesthetically occupied. Moreover, we must first enumerate that particular set of invariants which identifies the aesthetic mode of experience. Once we do this, however, it will then become possible to identify the specific form these features assume in each of the particular arts.

By recognizing that these experiential invariants are ubiquitous, certain important consequences follow. One of these is that art is continuous with other modes of experience. These invariants are a common denominator that make it impossible to separate art sharply from experiences of different sorts. This forces us to reject those views which would isolate art from life and the full spectrum of human activities. It is easier to quarantine the art object than the experience of it, and by focusing on the latter, the object is drawn back into the traffic of human intercourse. Another effect of acknowledging the unity of experience is that traditional notions of the passive and contemplative quality of aesthetic perception must be replaced by the active attention, involvement, and response of the participant in the aesthetic field. However, these and other consequences will become more apparent once we have specified these experiential features through a tentative description of the aesthetic field.

AESTHETIC ELEMENTS AND THEIR FUNCTIONS

There would appear to be simply two separate elements in the aesthetic field, the art object and the person who perceives it, with the object as the stimulus to which the perceiver responds. This, however, is so gross an oversimplification that it succeeds in falsifying more than in illuminating the characteristics of the

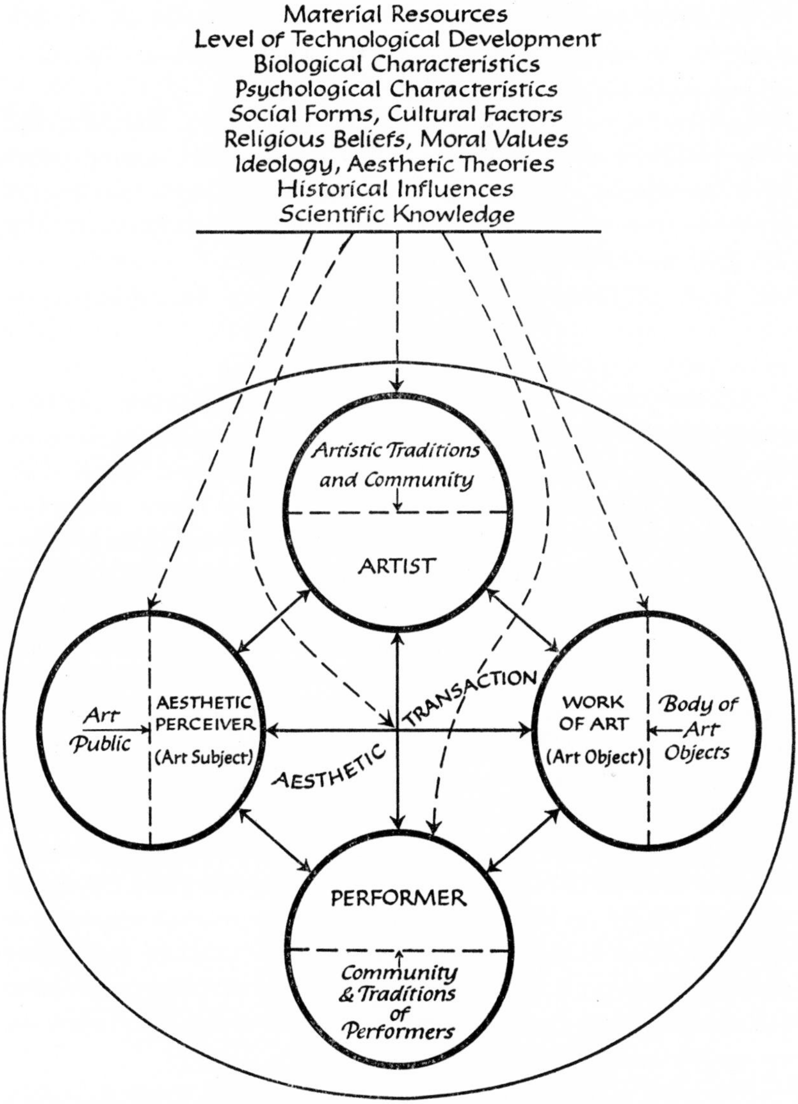

Material Resources
Level of Technological Development
Biological Characteristics
Psychological Characteristics
Social Forms, Cultural Factors
Religious Beliefs, Moral Values
Ideology, Aesthetic Theories
Historical Influences
Scientific Knowledge

FIGURE 2. The Aesthetic Field.

field. The art object and its perceiver, to be sure, do function in the aesthetic field, but in ways not explained or even suggested by the usual common sense account.

Let me first proceed by treating each of the main elements

in the situation, clarifying its place in the field and its relationships to the other elements. Then I shall examine the set of factors that exert a profoundly determining influence on all the elements in the field. It will become clear, however, that these elements and factors are actually inseparable and at points indistinguishable. Figure 2 offers an approximate isomorphic representation of the aesthetic field, and may help in making the discussion that follows somewhat clearer.

The Art Object

On the whole, it is likely that the greatest attention has been directed toward those objects we call collectively art, towards the painting, the poem, the sculpture, the musical score. Certainly this was the case before the rise of modern aesthetics, and it has continued as a major tradition. The kind of scholarship that has flourished in connection with the arts, for instance, seems to be concerned quite consistently with the historical investigation of art objects. Musicology, to take one example, is interested mainly in identifying the evolution of musical styles, techniques, notation, performance practices, and the like. Art history, to take another, devotes itself quite explicitly to research into the progression of movements and schools in the fine arts, and to stylistic characteristics and influences of individual artists and their periods. Whether or not scholarship in these and other arts proceeds historically, it is neither surprising nor unwelcome that the object of art has received this kind of attention. For surely any successful attempt to establish a body of knowledge about the arts must seek out those features that are most stable and open to common discussion. And these are exactly what the art object is capable of supplying.

The philosophy of art has taken much the same direction. It has searched for rules for the creation and judgment of art and for principles for understanding and explaining artistic practices. To illustrate and justify them, aesthetics has looked to those objects which seem to embody them. Rules for constructing and judging art objects have often been proposed—

rules like the three dramatic unities of time, place, and action, like the musical prohibition against leading voices in parallel fifths, like the Chinese "Rule of Five" for the patterning of visual elements, or like organic unity in poetry and the other arts. The concern of aesthetics with the features of the objects of art appears in the study of artistic form as the structural organization of elements or (as in significant form) as the effective use of the materials that are peculiar to a particular art. In a similar way, the analysis of artistic media and materials and the study of artistic styles direct attention toward objects.

Each of these object-centered concerns, however, can be interpreted in a more inclusive fashion. For no object is an independent or isolated element. The way in which we commonly refer to 'works' rather than 'objects' of art suggests that to direct attention exclusively to the object produces a partial and distorted result. Clearly, the art object is the work of someone; it is the product of the skillful activity of a creative artist. This is borne out in the very names we give them: painting, drawing, etching, sculpture, *objet trouvée*, movie, play, happening, symphony, sonata, song, opera, ballet, building, and the like. Such names reflect the process by which art objects are made rather than the forms they display when complete.[2] One is reminded here of Roger Fry's observation that "the drawn line is the record of a gesture." Thus its human origins cannot be disowned or ignored without losing an important source of illumination on the very object we wish to understand. So, too, does the object depend on the perceiver, on an individual or group that is receptive to its aesthetic potential. When we speak of a work of art in this connection, we are referring not to the art object alone but to the dynamic character of the aesthetic situation, which includes the active involvement as well as the passive receptivity of the person experiencing art. One might speak more accurately if more awkwardly of the "working" of art.

---

[2] Cf. Horace M. Kallen, *Art and Freedom* (New York, 1942), Vol. II, pp. 948-949 ff.

The object works on the percipient, and the percipient, in turn, actively works on the object.[3]

It may at first seem rather strange to speak of the object and the percipient as working on each other. Yet there is a reciprocal, functional relationship between them. The object is the center of attention in the aesthetic field, and it acts as the main stimulus of experience. It is the painting that captures our attention, the dramatic action that holds us, the music that envelopes and absorbs us. Still the perceiver must at the same time relate himself to the object. Through his active involvement he must vitalize the object by setting off its aesthetic potential. Thus the perceiver acts on the object in such ways as ordering and identifying the lines and figures of the painting, following and apprehending the plot of the play, and organizing music tones into melodic and harmonic patterns and recognizable thematic relationships.

The art object, then, is but the physical object or the event which contributes to the occasion of aesthetic experience by successfully functioning in the aesthetic field. It is not an intrinsic property of the object alone that determines whether it is art. Rather the entire object assumes that status as it functions aesthetically. The effect of time and distance on our willingness to accept objects of practical or religious use as artistic is an interesting instance of the functional dependence of the art object. The Greek vase, the prehistoric birdstone, the African ritual mask, and other such objects do not possess artistic stature through their intrinsic qualities; they rather acquire it when they become aesthetically accessible under changed conditions.

The physical limits of an object are not its experiential limits. When the object occurs as part of experience in the aesthetic

---

[3] Cf. Dewey ". . . (T)here is a difference between the art product . . . and the *work* of art. The first is physical and potential; the latter is active and experienced. It is what the product does, its working. . . . The *product* of art is not the *work* of art. The work takes place when a human being cooperates with the product so that the outcome is an experience that is enjoyed because of its liberating and ordered properties." (*Art as Experience*, pp. 162, 214.)

Stephen C. Pepper has made a highly sophisticated and illuminating analysis of the contextual status of the art object in "The Work of Art Described from a Double Dispositional Base," *The Journal of Aesthetics and Art Criticism*, XXIII, 4 (Summer 1965), pp. 421-7.

field, it only then truly becomes a work of art. The work of art in its fullest dimensions is, in the final analysis, the aesthetic transaction in its entirety. It is a transaction that occurs in the context of an environment involving, in minimal terms, an art object and an individual who activates its aesthetic potential. For it is essential to remember that the aesthetic field is a unity of experience and that identifying the percipient and the art object as elements in the field, as we have been doing in order to analyze it, disrupts the real coherence and integrity of the situation.

The actual functioning of the art object is a matter for empirical investigation. Certainly it varies with the different aesthetic dimensions that give every art form its own identity. And within each particular art, individual objects have their own peculiar combination of qualities. In painting, for example, the object is framed (or at least is stretched on a frame), and thus assumes physical discreteness as a surface having a single plane. Painting tends generally to direct our attention to rather finely detailed features of line, color, light and shadow, and composition, and, to a lesser extent, texture and mass. These qualities cause painting to function in particular ways. The range of distance and direction that the perceiver takes from the painting is severely limited, the requirements of lighting are fairly rigid, and the perceptual response is closely defined by the features of the painted surface. The kind of response that a perceiver makes is quite circumscribed by the pointillism of the impressionist Seurat, by the planes and solids of Cézanne, and by the eye-twisting configurations of the op artists, each in his own characteristic way.

In the related art of sculpture, some of the secondary qualities of painting tend to predominate. There is primary emphasis on volume and mass, on a third dimension and the increased range of movement of the perceiver that this demands. The planes and textures of surface assume greater importance, while color receives less. When we move from walk-in sculptures and environments to architecture, the functional dimensions of the art object shift again. Space becomes a central feature, both as it surrounds a perceiver who is within a building and as it confronts one who is without, when the structure is in spatial juxtaposition with its environment, whether of landscape, roads, or other buildings. Mass takes on renewed emphasis, and the texture and color of surface materials, and the changing relationships of light and shade play different roles from those they have in the other arts. The functional dependence of architecture on the perceiver (perhaps better called the inhabitant) appears through the important place that motion and time take in apprehending the range of physical dimensions, the changes in qualities of light during the course of the sun and the seasons, and the social uses which a building is designed to provide.

The characteristic qualities of the different media which each art uses also dictate the kind of object that it produces. The use of tempera, oil, or watercolor in painting results in objects with different perceptual qualities. So, too, is this the case when sculpture is made out of marble, bronze, clay, wood, or *objets trouvées,* and when a building is constructed out of earth, wood, marble, reinforced concrete, or aluminum and glass.

All the other arts can provide similar kinds of illustrations of the varying features of art objects, both in their material and in the ways in which they function in the aesthetic field. What is most needed, however, is to pursue systematically the task of describing the types and instances of art objects in the context of the functional role they play in the aesthetic field.

The Perceiver

While the art object has remained a subject of primary interest to the scholar and to the critic, the philosopher of art has, since the eighteenth century, often been preoccupied with the nature of the aesthetic response. By locating aesthetic experience in an "inner sense," and by centering attention on imagination, emotion, and sentiment, the eighteenth century British school shifted concern from the object to what may be called the psychology of aesthetic experience, and established aesthetics on the basis of a distinctive mode of experience.[4]

---

[4] Cf. the excellent discussion and documentation of this point in Jerome Stolnitz, "On the Origins of 'Aesthetic Disinterestedness,'" *The Journal of Aesthetics and Art Criticism,* XX, 2 (1961), 131-143.

The subsequent course of modern aesthetics has thus tended to direct itself to the question of the appropriate aesthetic attitude and the proper aesthetic response. Proposals for aesthetic disinterestedness, isolation, psychical distance and the like have been put forward as ways of characterizing the aesthetic attitude and setting it off from one that is scientific or cognitive, practical, moral, or religious. While there is no question of the historical importance of these concepts in contributing to the identification of an aesthetic mode of experience, it may be useful to reexamine them in the light of the manner in which the perceiver functions in the aesthetic field. For when these ideas are set against the phenomenology of aesthetic experience, the limitations imposed by their excessive concern with the psychology of attention becomes plain.

The tradition of modern empiricism, which dates from roughly the same time and place—seventeenth and eighteenth century England—has tended to construe experience as something that happens to a passive recipient. The sensationalistic empiricism of Locke, Berkeley, and Hume formed the dominant tradition and gave rise to what has been aptly called "the spectator theory of knowledge." Addison, in fact, in the very sequence of essays in which it has been claimed that modern aesthetics originated,[5] set forth the character of Mr. Spectator, a man who from infancy on assumed the role "rather as a Spectator of Mankind, than as one of the species," not as a participant in the affairs of the world but one who has acted throughout his life "as a looker-on."[6]

This conception of experience as something impinging upon men who are passive receivers has persisted unchallenged until recent times. While alternatives have been proposed from various directions, including pragmatism and Marxism, the traditional notion of experience as passive has retained its hold on aesthetic theory. It appears in the prevalence of such ideas as distance, disinterestedness, and isolation. I shall examine the latter two notions at some length in the following chapter. At this point, however, it would be useful to consider the special implications

-----

[5] Stolnitz, *op. cit.*, 143. Addison's papers on "The Pleasure of the Imagination" appeared in 1712 in the *Spectator*.

[6] Joseph Addison and Richard Steele, *The Spectator*, No. 1 (Addison).

and difficulties of the notion of distance for characterizing the attitude of the perceiver in the aesthetic field. For the idea of distance and its related concepts are symptomatic of a trend which persists in the writings of critics and philosophers and in the thinking of the artistic public.

It is quite usual for commentators who wish to set the experience of art apart from the practical activities of men to introduce such notions as detachment, distance, and contemplation as defining characteristics of aesthetic attention and experience. In his well-known and influential discussion of psychical distance, Edward Bullough[7] proposed the metaphorical use of the notion of distance to describe the attitude of detachment with which we appreciate art objects. This degree of psychological remove that we impose between ourselves and art objects enables us to set aside our practical attitude toward things. Bullough is able to cite a body of data which would seem to support the use of distance as an accurate descriptive concept. His examples include the tendency to disrupt this attitude of detachment in the aesthetic relationship when reference is made in art to sexual matters, when questions are raised regarding the validity of important social institutions and ethical sanctions, and when allusions are made to topical issues. Such things as these tend to diminish distance (i.e. to underdistance) so that the perceiver can no longer refrain from being personally caught up in the matter at hand instead of retaining a kind of aesthetic aloofness. There is, for Bullough, a corresponding excess of distance (i.e. overdistancing) which leads to total absence of personal involvement and hence to aesthetic irrelevance. But this, he adds, tends to turn into the more usual failing of underdistancing.

Hence, according to Bullough, the particular arts take account of this requirement of preserving distance by employing various devices and conventions. The literary arts make use of fantasy,

------

[7] " 'Psychical Distance' as a Factor in Art and an Esthetic Principle," *British Journal of Psychology*, V (1913), 87-118. The bulk of this paper has been reprinted in many anthologies, including Vivas and Krieger, eds. *The Problems of Aesthetics* (New York, 1953), pp. 396-405, and M. Rader, ed., *A Modern Book of Aesthetics*, 3rd ed. (New York, 1960), pp. 394-411.

unreality, and imagination, and they are essentially fictitious. Furthermore, they raise the possibility of censorship in cases where the public may not be entrusted to keep a sense of distance. The graphic arts, however representational they become, are at most an imitation of nature and not nature herself. And in theatre there are such devices as the arrangement and shape of the stage, the lighting, costumes, makeup, and stylized language; in sculpture, the absence of realistic color, and the use of pedestals; in painting, the framing of pictures and their two-dimensional character—all these appear to recognize the need to create in the perceiver an attitude sharply different from one of practical involvement.

Actually the idea of distance is not a new one in the history of philosophy, although the term may be. It draws, in fact, on a tradition that goes back at least as far as Plato and Aristotle, and reappears at many places and in many guises. For the notion of distance is a manifestation in modern aesthetics of the Aristotelian ideal of the contemplative attitude as man's greatest good, and of the Judeo-Christian ideal of the contemplative life. In Platonism, Neoplatonism, and Renaissance Platonism, the contemplative ideal possesses an aesthetic dimension. Moreover, the contemplative attitude was undoubtedly a major factor in the classical selection of the distance receptors of sight and hearing as the aesthetic senses.

All this is worth noting in order to point out that the hold which the concept of psychical distance possesses receives its sustenance from long and tenacious roots. And yet I would suggest that this is a prime example, despite appearances to the contrary, of the dependence of aesthetic thought on nonaesthetic and, indeed, nonexperiential factors. For the notion of psychical distance embodies a kind of aesthetic fastidiousness that does not do justice to the full range of pertinent data.

There has been good reason throughout the history of western civilization for the suspicion with which men have regarded the arts. Since Plato's day, art has been seen as a potential purveyor of sedition, of irreligion, of immorality, and of degeneration; and not without cause. The arts have satirized conventional beliefs, punctured smugness, condemned the oppressiveness, desperation, and injustice of a wide variety of human conditions. They have been used to rouse men to revolt, to harass conquerors, to regenerate traditions and social myths, and to illuminate human ideals. In the face of these uses of art, how, then, can we speak of distance? At best it is a limited notion, holding for selected instances. At worst it emasculates art of all relevancy and of its capacity as a force of vision and regeneration. How can concepts such as distance and contemplation do justice to the social involvement which generated the art of Daumier and Goya, the novels of Dickens and Dreiser, the depths and heights of the human spirit from *Guernica* to the finale of Beethoven's Ninth Symphony?

Indeed, the hold that distance has on our thinking suggests one reason that modern innovations in the arts have at first caused such distress to critics and public alike. For it is precisely this notion of removal that has impeded us in adapting to extensions in the range of aesthetic experience, and in hurdling the barriers that have traditionally been placed between the perceiver and the object of art. It is here that modern developments in the arts present the theory of art with both a major challenge and a liberating force. By making the perceiver's attitude rather than the object the central factor, they have extended the scope of aesthetic awareness to include objects and materials of all kinds, including those traditionally excluded from the fine arts. Yet by the choice of objects, the modern arts demand an attitude that is strikingly different from distancing. We are now confronted with shapes cut out of newspaper, with bits of cloth, mirror, hair, and other unlikely materials pasted onto canvas to form collages. We encounter assemblages made of kitchen utensils, bottles, and other useful objects of our mundane environment. We are faced with sculpture constructed from discarded machine parts, automobile bumpers, and other refuse of our commercial and industrial surroundings. Even pop art, painting that has retained the use of conventional materials, has taken for its subject matter the vulgar commercial products of our supermarkets and the glib stylizations of our comic strips. So, too, has music extended its vocabulary, now making use of traffic noises, footsteps, and the sound of dripping water; now choosing deliberately arranged strips of magnetic tape bearing electronically produced sounds. Literature uses the language of advertising copy, of street corner slang and gutter thought, and ruminates on the most ordinary things and events of daily life.

The breadth of appreciative response has been widened, too. There are environmental sculptures we must walk into or through. There are Happenings which have no audience in the traditional sense at all but in which the audience participates as performer. There is theatre-in-the-round which dispenses with the conventional proscenium arch and in which the audience can see itself past the players and in which the players emerge from and disappear into the audience. There is Brecht's theatre in which the players regularly turn around to inform or instruct the audience. There is optical art which twists the eye into responding to the painting, and surrealism which conjures up suggestive shapes and disconcerting juxtapositions from the hidden world of dreams and the unconscious. Moreover, functionalism in aesthetics has expanded to include the claims of the human personality as an essential component.[8]

These, in short, are highly pertinent data which aesthetics must account for. They cannot be dismissed as artistic aberrations. Such developments as these form a large share of what is most vital and influential in the artistic culture of western man today. Instead of being exceptions that can be shrugged off with *ad hoc* explanations that are attached indulgently to traditional theories like psychical distance, the roles must be reversed. It is the notion of distance which itself must be subordinated to the place of a special concept of limited application, if it is not discarded altogether.

To support this changed conception of the perceiver of art, there is a growing body of evidence, in addition to the practice of artists themselves, which comes out of research in the behavioral sciences. The psychology of art, in particular Gestalt

---

[8] Cf. Lewis Mumford, *Art and Technics,* esp. ch. 5, "Symbol and Function in Architecture," a plea for the humanizing function of architecture; and James Marston Fitch, "The Aesthetics of Function," *Annals of the New York Academy of Sciences,* Vol. 128, Article 2 (Sept. 27, 1965).

psychology, has demonstrated how the perceiver participates actively in the experience of artistic perception. The sociology of art is beginning to suggest the place of the arts as forces inciting and abetting social change. Cultural anthropology is illuminating the arts on the role they play in primitive ritual and in technological process and product. Many of these data are tentative, and the information they offer is more programmatic in significance than overwhelmingly convincing. Yet the direction in which they point is clear enough, and that is to an integration of the arts into the lives and purposes of men rather than to an experience of isolation in a region of special sensibility.

All this bears directly on the kind of account we must give of the perceiver's role in the aesthetic field. His is a place that is not independent or isolated, nor is he psychologically removed from being caught up in the experience of art. The new developments in the arts are evidence of a newly recognized aesthetic sensibility, rather than a new kind of artistic experience for which traditional theories are unable to account. Yet enlarging the range of aesthetic experience does not lose the contemplative equanimity of the past. It rather identifies what has always occurred in free aesthetic perception, and opens us to a fuller perceptual response to a wider range of objects. And what has the greatest pertinence here, the recognition of the broader and deeper scope of aesthetic experience enables aesthetic theory to establish itself on its own and not a borrowed foundation.

The Artist

The artist has always presented a special difficulty to traditional theories of art, for he appears to occupy an ambiguous position. He is, on the one hand, a technician, a craftsman in sound, line, color, or stone. He must master a large body of technical and theoretical information. He must develop skills, learning how to use a chisel or brush, mix colors, order tones and orchestrate them. At times he must be a careful planner in the use of his materials and a thoughtful organizer of objects and people. And in the case of the choreographer and the film director, the artist becomes a group leader. The artist, then, is an artisan, the original maker of an object.

On the other hand, the artist is the voice of the gods or even their rival. He works with excitement, groping his way into a virgin realm toward new regions of human sensibility where traditions and principles of the past no longer apply. His motive is the driving force of inspiration or the irrational compulsion of neurosis, and his goal is not known until he achieves it. The artist seems the paradigm of the perceiver, led on his way by forces independent of himself.

Yet mention of the perceiver provides a telling clue. From the ambiguous position of maker and appreciator, the artist comes to represent, in its full ranging form, the actual activity of aesthetic perception. Artistic creation involves more than producing an art object. It is the creation of conditions for aesthetic experience, and it becomes the prototype of aesthetic experience, both in its particular instances and in its general meaning. The conditions for such experience are the essential constituents of the aesthetic field, and it is these that the artist first calls into being. He does more than paint a picture, carve a statue, or set down verses. He introduces the art public to qualitative experience that has originality and uniqueness. This may have been what Rodin meant when he stated hyperbolically that "The artist never creates; he reveals." For the artist discovers as well as makes. He both invents and recognizes a new dimension of human sensibility, a sensibility which requires the presence of both independent material conditions as well as personal involvement. The result is a new experience of an aesthetic mode, one which reflects the form of the aesthetic field.

The artist himself, then, becomes a participant in the aesthetic field. As an experiencing person, he is an active perceiver of art. And as the originator of particular aesthetic experience, he becomes at times a source of information and explanation about it and of assistance in attaining it. For the artist's vision is the basis for perceptual emulation. We must know what his art is about, what the quality of experience is which he has seized upon and identified, before we can do anything further such as discuss, criticize, or judge the object he has made.

Here is where our knowledge of the genesis of an art object becomes important. There are many artistic occasions on which an awareness of the cultural situation in which a work was produced sensitizes our perception in a way that could not occur if we were to confine our attention to the art object alone. When we realize that Picasso found his theme for *Guernica*, for example, in the German bombardment of a tiny Spanish village during the Spanish Civil War, our awareness of the painting is increased. The presence of a bull in it, for example, becomes understandable. Bulls, or the symbolism of the bullfight, do not figure in the pathos of most wars. The painting becomes more than a depiction of the horrors of war in general; it takes on a particular significance through its association with a specific event. Perhaps this is one role that titles may play at times in the experience of art. They introduce a relationship or a setting which bears on the art object in order to influence and enhance our experience of the object itself.[9]

There are many other kinds of factors, too, of which our awareness can have a powerful effect on the experience of art. In some cases this may be knowledge of how an object was made. It makes a difference in our perception of sculpture, for instance, knowing whether the piece was produced by accretion or construction, or whether it was made by paring away excess material to reveal forms hidden underneath. For the texture of the surface and the configuration and structure of the object are often the direct outcome of the manner by which it was made. It makes a difference, too, when we know what materials were used, for each has its own peculiar sculptural properties. Henry Moore, for example, conceives his forms out of the material in which he is working. All this is so, despite the fact that the spatial abstractions that characterize sculpture remain the same in each instance.

Speaking more broadly, the technology of art is relevant to perception. While we can view paintings, for example, without knowing what the materials or techniques of application were, realizing this sensitizes us to the peculiar qualities of the end

---

[9] This point is made effectively in F. David Martin, "Naming Paintings," *The Art Journal*, XXV, 3 (Spring 1966), 252-6.

result. The Venetians' application of oil paint in layers of thin glaze produces a depth and glow which is an effect peculiar to this medium and technique. The same is true of the impasto technique of Van Gogh and Karl Appel, applying the pigment thickly with heavy brush strokes or with a palette knife. The technology of art makes available at different times various materials and the techniques which they permit, and each material produces its own peculiar effect. Watercolor leads to an art that is swift, spontaneous, and straightforward, for no corrections are possible. Tempera is quite different in its qualities, for it is a technique that uses a mixture of pigment and egg yolk which dries quickly and cannot be darkened without loss of intensity. Consequently, tempera painting must be planned completely in advance. It also encourages simple areas of color, since the pigment cannot be manipulated on the surface of the painting; and this imposes restrictions on the way in which contours can be modeled. Because the range of values is restricted from full hue to white, the painter must reverse the order we observe in our daily perception. He is obliged to use the full hue for shadows and lighter values for convexities, while in normal vision the outstanding areas would have the full intensity of the hue and the more distant areas the lighter values.

A painting, then, is no timeless object. It is a product of skillful making, and it is making which is conditioned by the technology available to the artist. The picture is the product of its process, and understanding that process makes us see the painting differently—with greater fullness, range and acuity. Similar examples can be drawn as readily from any of the other individual arts.

Much the same case can be made from the way in which our perception is influenced when we know that an artist held a stylistic or aesthetic theory such as cubism, impressionism, futurism, or serialism. Such knowledge often does more than influence our perception; it may indeed make it possible. The same holds true for those art objects in which symbolism is an inherent part of the style and is not introduced *ab extra* to meet the demands of a critic's or aesthetician's theory. In symbolist poetry or Hindu dance, for example, it is essential to know the stylistic intent of the poet, the materials of the tradition, the import of the different gestures and stances, to be able to have full aesthetic apprehension. Similarly, our understanding of the artist's intention, if we can discover what it is, may contribute not a basis for judging an object but rather a source of insight into its features and qualities. In the final analysis, though, it is wise to keep D. H. Lawrence's admonition in mind: "Never trust the teller, trust the tale."

It is, however, in a common activity that the line between artist and perceiver begins to disappear, and the two merge with one another. The process of appreciation is actually a super-imposition on the process of creation, for both reflect the common process of experiencing that the aesthetic field describes analytically. The sculptor George Segal has observed that "All art comes from a life experience," and art becomes the deliberate handling of such experience in an effort to capture and hold a unique perception of it. The material, style, and structure of experience become the qualitative stuff out of which art is made.

Even in his etymology, the artist is a maker, and the poetics of his art is the theory of its making. It is by means of what Valéry calls a *"synthèse artificielle"* that an art object is "fabricated."[10] Stravinsky, in fact, calls himself an "inventor of music."[11] Indeed, this very activity of making has, in recent times, taken over to become in some instances the dominant motif of an art object. Here one thinks of the action painting of de Kooning and Pollack, of Pirandello's plays about themselves, of Happenings created in some measure out of themselves as they proceed, of aleatoric music which introduces a chance element into the process of composition or performance, of films concerned with themselves, as in the case of Fellini's 8½, and of Gide's novel in process, *The Counterfeiters.*

The artist, then, is an integral part of the aesthetic field. He originates an experience which may thereafter be repeated in kind. And he participates in what is essentially a common human involvement in the field.

------

[10] Paul Valéry, *Poésie et pensée abstraite.*
[11] *Poetics of Music* (New York, Vintage Books, 1956), p. 54.

The Performer

The performing arts introduce what perhaps is an unwelcome complexity into traditional aesthetic theories. For the performer seems to compromise the genius and authority of the composer, playwright, or choreographer. Instead of being an important but impersonal intermediary, the performer often interposes his personality and usurps the central position of the creative artist. Seldom is he a reflection of what the artist intended, a neutral transmitter to the audience of what is in the score or script. Indeed, the performer often obscures through his virtuosity the very object he should be conveying to the perceiver. Furthermore, he usually succeeds in disturbing the perceiver's contemplative equanimity, making it difficult to dissociate himself and maintain the distance necessary for proper appreciation. If all this is the case, then, one can understand why the performer is often accounted for by denying his importance, by making him into a necessary but irrelevant distraction from the proper communion between the artist and his public.

Yet one is justly wary of explanation by denial. The fact that certain arts depend for their realization upon being performed does indeed force a complicating circumstance on us. And yet it is one that may be welcome. For instead of confusing the issue, the performer makes us face the fact that art is an experience that is active, a process of doing something that involves knowledge and skill, and an activity that is social at heart. The performing artist is no intruder into the normally direct communion between artist and perceiver. Rather he emphasizes what is always there, an active handling of the perceptual materials of the arts and an alert receptivity to them that require a duration of time for development and completion. This is the case with all the arts, irrespective of whether or not they require a performer. Those that do not simply consolidate his role with that of the perceiver. Let me develop and illustrate these ideas by turning to some specific arts.

In discussing the individual arts, we must recognize that each possesses qualities and attributes that are peculiar to it and that make it distinctive. The characteristics that identify an art are a complex of features, and this makes it difficult to classify the arts into a neat arrangement according to the sense they appeal to or the material out of which they construct their objects. Thus it is that a descriptive account of the aesthetic field will vary in many particulars from one art to the next, and each account must be governed by a careful examination of the actual functioning of the art on its own terms. Not only will each art probably reveal its own characteristic version of the aesthetic field, but variations of the field will undoubtedly appear as we examine different artistic styles, historical periods, and movements. The use of distance to characterize the appreciative experience varies, as we have already noted, with the art and the object we are considering. It is much less applicable to an appreciation of Beethoven's *Moonlight Sonata* than of the Taj Mahal or a Constable landscape.

The task of discerning the modal transformations of the aesthetic field from one art to the next is the job of the aesthetician and the historian of the arts and of culture. And it is the job of the critic to perceive with sensitivity and discernment the way in which a particular art object functions in its own peculiar fashion in the aesthetic field. All this affects our discussion of the individual arts. Yet the larger point with which we are concerned here is that the basic structure of the aesthetic field remains constant throughout all the arts, and that the performer represents a generic feature of the aesthetic field rather than a peculiar feature of certain arts only. Let me press this contention by looking more closely at two arts, music, which is nominally a performing art, and poetry, which is not.

Until recent times the composer's product was always incomplete. The score he wrote was far removed from the materials of his craft—sound and silence in movement. In order for a musical object to be produced, the written notation had to be translated into aural qualities by means of physical instruments designed for that purpose and manipulated by players skilled in their use. Often, in fact, the roles of composer and performer were combined in the same person, and their functions were associated with each other. Nearly all the major composers of the eighteenth and nineteenth centuries were accomplished instrumentalists, usually pianists, who were easily capable of realizing as sound the musical ideas they had thought and written. Performance thus was an indispensable adjunct to composition, both of them combining to produce the musical event.

Now the situation appears to have changed radically. It might seem as if modern technology has made the musical performer extraneous and dispensable. The development of high fidelity audio equipment has made it possible to reproduce at will a vast array of musical works with such remarkable fidelity that the aural effect is difficult to distinguish from what it would be at a live performance. Indeed the claim is sometimes made that the results of a good sound reproduction system are far superior to an actual performance. There is no coughing and rattling of programs to distract the listener, and tonal balance is at an optimum instead of being subject to the acoustical vagaries of a concert hall and the location of one's individual seat. In recording, mistakes in the execution of music can neatly be cut out of the tape and a perfect version spliced in. In fact, the invention of magnetic recording tape has made possible the use of electronic instruments such as the RCA Music Synthesizer by means of which the composer can create directly on tape whatever qualities and combinations of sounds he desires, and thus dispense entirely with the need ever to have his work performed by another. Or if he prefers, he can splice together previously recorded strips of tape, or otherwise prepare his own composition directly on the tape. Thus it is possible to eliminate the many variables of performance which result from the fact that only the main details can ever be notated, and that a wide range of subtle features have to be left to the performer's discretion or to chance.

It might seem, then, that in one fashion or another the musical performer has become technologically obsolete. These developments, however, are but part of the relevant data. While they cannot be dismissed by branding them as evidence of the decline of modern culture, they are at the same time balanced and even overshadowed by a remarkable resurgence in musical performance. The striking growth of applied music in school curricula, of amateur and semiprofessional orchestras, of chamber music concert series and amateur associations, of summer music festivals and the like, all testify to an enlarged public for live performances as well as for recorded ones. Performance is thus sought after as a viable form of musical experience, and aesthetic theory must account for it. The nonperformance types of musical experience, on the other hand, can be dealt with in the same fashion as the arts that do not rely upon performance at all. Exactly what, then, is the place of performance in the musical mode of the aesthetic field?

As an art, music tends to be misleading. The intangibility of musical materials has often attracted those who seek mystical or spiritual experiences. Music has long served as a useful illustration and confirmation for metaphysical idealism, and the philosophical rationalist has consistently recognized the close analogy that can be drawn between mathematics and music, discovering in music a perfect vehicle by which to pass from the rational universe to the sensory realm. Music has also had other uses—for the romantic who finds in it a means for engaging in the life of feeling, for the sensualist who can respond with delight to the caressing of sound, for the dreamer who receives from music a stimulus for reverie.

Yet these are misleading. All such uses of music illustrate the deeply rooted propensity to refuse to take this and every other art in the fullness of their own features. Instead, the arts are used as a means of satisfying psychological needs that are quite apart from their aesthetic function (however legitimate such demands may be in their own right). Or they become a convenient opportunity for supporting an intellectual commitment that is quite independent of the arts.

The musical experience of the concert or recital hall is something quite different from what is usually said about it. Of all the arts, it is music which lends itself most readily to an uncommitted examination. Unlike the fine and theatrical arts, it does not mislead one by a resemblance to the appearance or action of things that have a life independent of the arts. And unlike the literary arts, music does not use materials that have a regular use apart from their artistic one. For music employs materials, forms, and productive techniques contrived especially for that purpose, and these are only tangentially related to the world outside of the musical arts. Music, thus, demands to be taken in its own terms.

When we attempt to do this, some very interesting results develop. First, we discover that we cannot describe the musical experience by sound and silence alone. The musical field is a complex situation containing a number of significant elements and factors.[12] There is, for instance, a powerful element of spectacle in the musical event. Musical performance possesses a visual presence which is not at all a distraction from the medium of pure sound but rather adds a dramatic quality to the occasion. The sight of a large symphony orchestra guided and controlled by its conductor, of the members of a string quartet working responsively to achieve an harmonious interplay of sounds, of a solo recitalist joining with his instrument to produce a continuous tonal line or pattern—these possess a relevance that far transcends the mechanical function of producing sound. Perhaps most important is the demand that the listener constantly humanize the musical experience, that he realize its complete dependence on the ability of people to work in the materials and with the instruments of the musical act in order to understand and to create in experience the written indications of the composer. The full musical experience betrays the falsity of amputating the product from the process of artistic making. It forces us to see the intimate connection between making music and perceiving it. In fact, it helps us see these as forms of the same basic activity, joining together the performer, the listener, and the composer. By participating sympathetically in the activity of performance, the listener identifies with what is going on and achieves genuine participation in the field of musical experience.[13]

----

[12] A more detailed criticism of the practice of reducing each art to a single sense through which it is held to work appears in my paper, "The Sensuous and the Sensual in Aesthetics," *J. of Aesthetics and Art Criticism*, XXIII, 2 (Winter 1964), 185-192.

[13] This identification appears quite clearly in the folk arts of diverse cultures. Amadou Sissoko, for example, writing on the art of African Ballet, the national folk dance company of Liberia, has commented that in Africa, "more than anywhere else the professional is an amateur, a performer particularly gifted

The theatrical aspect of musical performance contributes in other ways to the musical experience. By correlating sight with sound, it facilitates the act of attention, and makes it easier for the listener to notice and follow what is happening. Obviously the visual spectacle can be a distraction, and sometimes this danger is abetted by the performer. Yet when it is a successful adjunct to the musical experience, the visual aspect of the live performance assists attention more than it seduces it. Music cut off from its production, as in radio or recorded performances, requires an extraordinary act of concentration to avoid becoming a stimulus to trains of thought totally unconnected with the sounds themselves. Indeed it is clear that this inclination is frequently indulged deliberately, and the musical event becomes no art at all but rather an occasion for conversation, reading, or work. Recorded music tends to make us forget another essential feature of the musical experience, that it is a social experience. The musical event is a social event; it is an occasion of people coming together to make and listen to music. Music is not an experience that occurs in inner isolation to a sequestered consciousness. It involves people in groups, using the mechanical, structural, and organizational products of human technology— musical instruments, concert halls, and the more or less elaborate network of concert management. All these have varying degrees of relevance, and it is a narrowness of vision that so compart- mentalizes the musical event as to extrapolate one fragment and exhibit it as the whole. It is indeed possible to regard records as what they are literally called—records of musical events that help to preserve these past occurrences and serve as aural reminders of the live events in the full range of their experience.

But while recordings are valuable as musical documents and as didactic devices, they unfortunately can not duplicate the creative immediacy of the ongoing musical act, when the present is actively growing out of what has gone before and the future is not yet done. For there is an element of performance present in the actual musical event, an ongoing movement of qualitative

---

who has the ability to create around himself the effective participation of all the 'Bara' (the traditional circle of song and dance which is analogous to the audience in Europe). The limit is then difficult to establish between the artist and the spectator."

experience which involves the active handling of perceptual materials and the alert receptivity of all those who are part of it. And all this takes place within a creative duration of time through which it develops and comes to completion.[14]

Because the account of performance bears directly on the main theme of this study, let me consider an art usually regarded as nonperforming, the art of poetry. Here, too, this characterization of poetry is incomplete. For in its very beginnings and throughout its early history, poetry was an art that involved performers, participants, and audience. The evidence we have seems to show that when poetry arises in the folk culture of a society it is recited or sung. The early Greek epics, for example, were written to be recited, their lyric poems were composed to be sung to the accompaniment of a musical instrument, usually a lyre, and in nearly all cultures drama emerges out of religious ritual as a literary form written to be acted. The same seems to be true of the ballad, which arose as a narrative poem intended to be sung, coming, according to one theory, out of the collective activity of a social group singing and dancing together. The medieval *roman* and *chanson de geste*, too, were composed by troubadours and trouvères and recited or sung to audiences.

These observations on the early development of poetry settle nothing about the character of the art in modern times. Still they force us to recognize certain relationships between poetry and music, resemblances that suggest generic similarities rather than accidents of origin. And they enable us to view the elements of performance associated with poetry today as more than deviations from the norm. In addition to the survival of performance in the renewed popularity of folk songs and ballads and in dramatic forms such as musical comedy and, perhaps, opera, where language may assume importance, there is increasing interest in poetry readings, live and recorded, which carry on the early tradition of the art.

Yet even apart from overt performance, the experience of poetry compresses performance and appreciation into the same

---

[14] The extent to which the active musical event has been denied by removing it from its temporal context of process is illustrated by a recent writer who sees music, in the form of the plastic record disc, entering the higher spatial realm of tangible physical objects!

activity. Poetry is a deliberate art, deliberate in its creation and deliberate in its appreciation. This is no comment on the method of poetic composition but rather on the quality of the poetic materials. There is an element of care in poetry, an absence of what is superfluous and a reduction to only that which is essential. This deliberateness is an essential feature shared by both the creative and the appreciative involvement with poetry. It appears in the poetic sensibility in at least two ways, in the elements of song that vitalize the language of poetry, and in the imagery which is the special substance of poetic thought.

Poetic song is true music. Poetry speaks to us with the silent voice of imagination, but with no less a voice for that. Mallarmé's remark to Degas is to the point: "Now, Degas, verses are not made with ideas, but with words." The sounds of phonemes work together to create a musical fabric which the poet deliberately weaves through the considered arrangement of consonance, assonance, alliteration, and varying patterns of rhyme. Sounds combine with another musical element, rhythm, which appears in the pattern of accented and unaccented syllables in poetic feet, in the pattern of feet, accents, and ideas in a line, and in the arrangement of verses in a stanza and stanzas in a poem. These rhythmic pulses of different dimensions combine to create a parade of movement to accompany the sounds of poetry. Poetic experience includes an acute awareness of these features of poetic song, and this is something that increases with close acquaintance and thoughtful reading.

Imagery, too, is literally evocative, calling out through original and vivid associations a fresh awareness of our experience. Yet this very power of figurative language is something that must be discovered and exercised. Poetic experience demands of us an active and thoughtful receptivity. We must understand and think through the metaphors in order to experience a poem, and this demands considered and informed reading, which in turn requires that we develop the knowledge and skill to do this. Such preparation is not unlike that of the performer, only here the performer and the listener are telescoped into the same person. Indeed, the successful teaching of a poem consists in enabling one to interpret it actively, that is, to perform it effectively for oneself.[15] It becomes clear, then, that there is a performing element in the demands that poetic experience makes on the reader. He must become a performer if he is to engage the poem successfully. Valéry confirms this when he notes, "It is the performance of the poem which is the poem. Without this, these rows of curiously assembled words are but inexplicable fabrications."[16]

Now what is true of poetry can, I think, be shown to hold for the other "nonperforming" arts, each in its own way. Even painting and sculpture require experience with the medium and, if they are representational, the recognition of their images. Traces of their origin confront us, whether it be through brush strokes, chisel marks, or the dribble or slash of action painting. And these lead to the demand for knowledge of artistic techniques, history, and other influences our awareness of which will enhance and develop our perception.

The performing activity, then, is not aesthetically superfluous, nor is it an unwelcome complication to the aesthetic field. Much to the contrary, the function of performance is an integral feature of the experience of art, and it occupies a place in the aesthetic field as an essential phase of that experience. When the field is regarded as a unity in experience, the varying functions of object, perceiver, artist, and performer are indissolubly connected and interdependent, although the particular distribution of these functions will vary with the art, the object, and the perceiver. The contrast between the unity of experience and the varying structure of the aesthetic field is the difference between art and the theory of art.

----

[15] The view that the poetic experience is central is sometimes attacked on the grounds that such experience is mental. And being mental, it ends in complete subjectivism and skepticism, since there would be no way of judging among competing interpretations. (Cf. for example, Rene Wellek and Austin Warren's *Theory of Literature.*) The answer to this objection is clear. The experience of poetry is not subjective since it is not exclusively psychological. And the demands of the poetic object in the aesthetic field clearly render some interpretations better than others by allowing the object to function more fully and effectively in the total, integrated experience. But more of this in Chapter V, where I shall consider aesthetic judgment and criticism more fully.

[16] Paul Valéry, "The Course in Poetics: First Lesson." In B. Ghiselin, *The Creative Process* (New York, New American Library, 1955), p. 99.

FACTORS CONDITIONING THE AESTHETIC FIELD

This analysis of the aesthetic field has attempted to do full justice to its variability for different arts, objects, and perceivers, as well as to its structural uniformity. Yet art is not a precious isolate in the lives of men. It is rather a dimension of experience that works within the full range of human activity, and thus affects and is affected by the same sorts of things that condition all human experience. Moreover, the same variability that occurs among specific instances of aesthetic experience occurs in, and indeed because of, the factors that influence the field. It will be helpful to look more closely at these factors, although what I can say here will be only tentative and suggestive. The task of detailing the specific fashion in which these elements influence the aesthetic field calls for specialized investigation in each of the disciplines involved.

Biological Factors

The aesthetic field is a perceptual field. Yet it is a field not of visual and auditory experience alone but one which invokes the full range of sensory responses of which the human organism is capable. Visual, tactile, auditory, olfactory, gustatory, and kinaesthetic perceptions are involved in aesthetic as in all other normal experience. But there is more. There is full somatic participation in aesthetic experience involving such things as respiration, heartbeat, skin state, muscular flexings, and rhythmical movement. This is no passive condition; the perceiver is sharply aware both in his senses and in his body. Indeed, there is a kind of general bodily sensing. The biological basis of aesthetic perception is fundamental.

Since the experience of art is a natural one that possesses physical and biological aspects, those traits of the human organism that affect this mode of experience have real bearing on our understanding and analysis of the aesthetic field. Biological characteristics of the human organism impose upper and lower limits on the intensity of stimulation, and they determine the manner in which we perceive physical events. For example, sensory overloading and deprivation have an equally deleterious effect on the body. Too great stimulation first obstructs balanced judgment and then rationality itself. On the other hand, experimental subjects isolated from all visual, thermal, haptic and sonic stimulation "were reduced to gibbering incoherence in a matter of a few hours."[17]

All normal experience, including aesthetic, must occur within these limits of sensory stimulation, and such limits can be specified for each of the sensory channels. Auditory perception, for instance, normally takes place between 20 and 20,000 vibrations per second. This range is about 10 octaves, the most useful part of which is spanned by the piano which extends 7¼ octaves from A-27½ to C-4186. The overtones of each fundamental pitch whose frequencies are between 4,000 and 10,000 and above allow us to identify the peculiar timbre of different instruments. Between 16 and 20 vibrations per second are necessary for us to begin to perceive a sound as continuous. Similarly, the eye cannot perceive radiation below 3200 Angstroms, and motion pictures create the illusion of continuous movement when the speed of projection presents about 16 frames to the eye per second (although this is increased to 24 frames per second to eliminate objectionable flickering).[18]

Human biology also assigns conditions to the time span within which we are capable of perceiving and responding with alertness, as well as to the manner in which variations in the quality and intensity of sensation influence the range of that temporal continuum. And while the body tends to seek a psychosomatic equilibrium, it seeks an equilibrium which is nonetheless dynamic. For instance, in the case of many odors, some aspects of touch, and "white" sound, exposure to steady stimulation at some fixed level will ultimately deaden perception.[19]

Other biological characteristics also affect aesthetic perception. The fact that the human organism is capable of total feedback, a trait it shares with other land mammals which makes it capable of perceiving the stimuli it produces, bears heavily on aesthetic perception as well as on human communication.[20] Indeed, this provides biological corroboration of the

[17] James Marston Fitch, "The Aesthetics of Function," pp. 707-8.
[18] Wilmer T. Bartholomew, *Acoustics of Music* (New York, 1942), pp. 201-3.
[19] Fitch, *op. cit.*, p. 708.
[20] Bernard Berelson and Gary A. Steiner, *Human Behavior, An Inventory of Scientific Findings* (New York, 1964), pp. 46-47.

essential unity of human participation in the aesthetic field by perceiver, artist, and performer. Moreover, the human body, occupying and moving through space, establishes relationships to its environment which are a function of its physiological characteristics. Man is a "perceptual-motor being-in-the-world" rather than a creature restricted largely to "cerebral-visual seeing."[21] Indeed, the total bodily perception and response to its environment becomes a central fact in the aesthetics of every art. In architecture, for example, this means that there are only participants, no spectators.[22]

Such considerations as these make it clear that a primary influence on the nature of the aesthetic field arises from the physical attributes and abilities of the human organism, together with the changing ways in which he can fashion things in his environment to function in relation to him. Often this biological component is directly apparent in our encounter with art. Houseman's remark on the definition of poetry is one instance: "Poetry indeed seems to me more physical than intellectual. . . . I could no more define poetry than a terrier can define a rat, but . . . we both recognized the object by the symptoms which it provokes in us. . . ."[23]

Psychological Factors

Psychological factors comprise a multidimensional influence on the aesthetic field which covers at least three major areas: the psychology of perception, the psychology of appreciation (or the aesthetic attitude), and the psychology of artistic creation. It is not my purpose here to assume the large burden of reviewing the literature in the psychology of art. What is necessary is rather to identify the bearing which psychological inquiry has on our understanding of the aesthetic field.

The kind of perceptual experience that takes place in the complex set of relationships between the perceiver and the

---

[21] Tarmo Pasto, *The Space-Frame Experience in Art* (New York, 1964), pp. 15-16.

[22] Fitch, *op. cit.*, p. 706.

[23] A. E. Houseman, *The Name and Nature of Poetry.* In B. Ghiselin, ed., *op. cit.*, p. 90.

object of art has a powerful effect on aesthetic experience. For this reason the psychology of perception bears significantly on the analysis of the aesthetic field. By identifying characteristic patterns of perceptual experience, it may become possible to explain and even eventually to predict and to judge art in particular cases. Both behaviorist and Gestalt psychology have already contributed to our understanding of aesthetic perception.

We are aware, for example, of the need for differentiated sensory input, and of how sensitivity to sensation varies with the increase and decrease of input.[24] Psychologists have also identified the "phi phenomenon" on which moving pictures are based, the apparent motion that results from alternating two successive but slightly different visual stimuli.[25] This can be observed in music, too, when rapidly repeated notes are heard as a continuous and intense sound, a phenomenon long put to practical use in orchestrating music through the use of the tremolo.

Gestalt psychology has found the arts fertile ground for working out patterns of visual perception. The gestaltists have identified principles of visual organization concerning the figure-ground relationship, grouping, closure, sensory fusion, sequence principles, and "good" figures. They have shown how such factors as ambiguity and familiarity affect our interpretation and judgment in literature and the fine arts. In efforts such as these, we can get beyond subjectifying art and move toward stabilizing aesthetic experience in a perceptual process involving the interdependence of the observer and the observed object.[26] Whether from a behavioral or gestaltist point of view, there seems to be agreement on this contextual relationship.[27] One psychologist

---

[24] Cf. Berelson and Steiner, *op. cit.*, pp. 89, 91.

[25] *Op. cit.*, p. 99.

[26] Cf. Rudolf Arnheim, *Art and Visual Perception* (Berkeley and Los Angeles, 1954), p. viii.

[27] Cf. the rather graphic description by the behaviorist B. F. Skinner: "The perceiver apprehends the world almost as one apprehends a criminal. He makes it his own almost as if he were ingesting it, as one ingests the body of a god in the rites of Mithra. He knows the world almost in the biblical sense of possessing it sexually." "The Problem of Consciousness—A Debate. Reply by Professor Skinner," *Philosophy and Phenomenological Research*, XXVII, 3 (March 1967), p. 327.

sums all this up quite well when he observes that "Both biology and psychology lend support to the view that the aesthetic is a feeling for right adjustments as opposed to faulty."[28]

The psychology of appreciation is in a less developed stage than the psychology of perception. Yet it too has the potential of contributing significantly to our knowledge of the function of the perceiver in the aesthetic field. Unfortunately appreciation has not lent itself to experimental inquiry as readily as has perception. This is partly because the treatment of appreciation is influenced greatly by the particular theory of art that is assumed rather than by observation and experimentation. It also results from the fact that whatever investigation has been done rests in large part on interviews and questionnaires, and consequently the conclusions that are drawn are far more apt to be influenced by the respondent's *a priori* ideas about proper appreciation than by his actual appreciative experiences. And such ideas also have their source in philosophical speculation and in nonaesthetic convictions.

I tried to show earlier how these influences have contributed to the widespread use of the notion of distance for characterizing the proper attitude of appreciation. There are still other attributes commonly ascribed to the aesthetic attitude which have rarely if ever been questioned, as when it is said to be contemplative, intrinsic, and disinterested. In the chapters that follow we shall inquire more closely into these notions. In general, they tend to originate in philosophical commitments, yet properly they should be judged by psychological investigations of artistic practice and experience. It is, in fact, necessary to cull the empirical from the conceptual in any discussion of the aesthetic attitude in order to see precisely which aspects of appreciation are amenable to empirical testing and which result from a conceptual or theoretical decision.

A preliminary step to the experimental treatment of the psychology of appreciation would be to survey, classify, and analyze the various descriptions that have been given of the aesthetic attitude. Professor Stolnitz has identified four definitions of the aesthetic attitude that appear in modern aesthetic

---

[28] R. M. Ogden, *The Psychology of Art* (New York, 1938), p. 22.

theory. He sees it defined "(1) in terms of *purpose*: there is no 'interest' ulterior to the act of perception itself; (2) in terms of *attention*: there is close attention to the qualitative individuality of what is perceived; (3) in terms of *belief*: 'a consciousness of the difference between appearance and reality is lacking' or, the percipient is aware of the difference between appearance and reality; (4) *semiotically*: the aesthetic object is not or does not function as a sign."[29]

This sort of classification is useful, for it locates the central issues that have been raised by attempts to formulate the aesthetic attitude. Using some such classification, we can analyze the definitions in order to determine the kinds of features each possesses, and the evidence that supports each feature. What may very well emerge is that each of these definitions of the aesthetic attitude can be ('and has been) offered out of a combination of philosophical assumption, introspective insight, stipulation, and cursory observation. What is needed for an experimental approach to the psychology of appreciation, however, is to appraise and justify any proposed definition on the grounds of experimental testing. The task of an experimental aesthetics, then, is clearly first to identify empirically the defining characteristics of that mode of experience we call aesthetic, and, second, to try and discover what are the psychological attributes of the perceiver in aesthetic experience. Working in this way, we can hope to reach firm ground on which to construct aesthetic theory, and thus end the interminable debate that has dogged the heels of speculative aesthetics.

The failure to establish experimentally what the characteristics of aesthetic experience are has limited the value of attempts like that of Bullough to classify "perceptive types." On the basis of his experiments with the perception of color in isolation and in combination, Bullough classified four types of percipients: associative (in which the percipient has emotional associations, either distinct from the feeling tone of color or fused with it), physiological (in which the percipient judges color by the reactions, especially the organic ones, it causes in him),

---

[29] Jerome Stolnitz, "Some Questions Concerning Aesthetic Perception," *Philosophy and Phenomenological Research*, XXII, 1 (Sept. 1961), 87.

objective (in which the percipient directs his attention exclusively to an analysis of the object, making no reference to his personal responses), and character (in which the percipient projects his responses and sees them as features of the object.)[30] This same classification scheme has been applied by others to musical compositions, rectangular forms, pictures, and poetry.[31]

Several questions arise about this sort of experimental treatment of the aesthetic attitude, questions that have to do with the stimulus object, the perceptual relationship, and the classification of attitudes. In the first place, an individual color (or sound) differs considerably from an object in the visual arts, although one can understand the experimental advantages of stimulus simplicity. Legitimate doubts persist about the extent to which results that are obtained with such stimuli can be said to reflect and illuminate the perception of art objects. Moreover, this relationship between a perceiver and a particular stimulus is an extrapolation from the full situation in which art is experienced and differs sharply from it. The question can be raised about whether taking art appreciation out of the context of the aesthetic field can give us accurate data on which to base a classification of attitudes. Yet another difficulty arises from Bullough's attempt to classify all the types of responses that are made to the stimuli. By accepting all the responses as equally legitimate, he overlooks the prior need to identify first the aesthetic quality of experience, against which the aesthetic relevance of the responses can be measured. This applies also to his ranking of the four types of percipients (the most aesthetic is "character," descending through "fused associative," "objective," "nonfused associative," to "physiological"). This ranking is itself not experimentally established but rather reflects Bullough's acceptance of a conception of the aesthetic attitude in

---

[30] Edward Bullough, "The 'Perceptive Problem' in the Aesthetic Appreciation of Simple Colour-Combinations," *British Journal of Psychology*, III (1910), 406-447.

[31] Cf. the discussion of these studies and bibliographical references in Jerome Stolnitz, *Aesthetics and Philosophy of Art Criticism* (Boston, 1960), pp. 54, 77-81, and in C. W. Valentine, *The Experimental Psychology of Beauty* (London, 1962), pp. 53 ff.

which distance is the central feature and the criterion for ranking.[32]

Rather than ranking the percipients *after* classification on the basis of a prior definition of the aesthetic attitude that is stipulated nonexperimentally, we must *first* determine the type and characteristics of response that are relevant by reference to the mode of aesthetic experience, and then appraise our experimental results. It is indeed possible to raise serious doubts about the basic assumption that the aesthetic attitude (like aesthetic experience) is a unique or special one at all. It may, in fact, be an attitude that shares many features in common with other types of perception, yet differing by being quantitatively more intense or by combining ordinary properties in a typical way.[33] In any case, the persistence of nonempirical assumptions and fragmented data has limited the value of much experimental work. While problems such as these dog the efforts of the psychology of art to become experimental, they do not prevent it. They rather show the close association in which the philosophy and the psychology of art must work.

When we turn to the psychology of artistic creation, we enter a region that has been beset by numerous problems and confusions of its own. The creation of art, perhaps more than anything else connected with art, has been obscured by a

---

[32] "Its freedom from purely personal factors, from accidental memories and irrational associations, and its essentially emotional tone invest this type with a kind of objective reality, which is generally characteristic of aesthetic experiences, and stamps this form of colour-appreciation as the *aesthetic* appreciation *par excellence.*" Edward Bullough, "The 'Perceptive Problem' in the Aesthetic Appreciation of Single Colours," *British Journal of Psychology,* II (1907), 463.

[33] In a recent discussion of the aesthetic attitude ("The Myth of the Aesthetic Attitude," *American Philosophical Quarterly,* I, 1 (1964), 56-65), George Dickie rejects distance and disinterestedness as distinguishing characteristics, and then concludes that identifying it as a distinctive attitude is theoretically (although not historically or practically) useless. However, it does not follow that by eliminating distance and disinterestedness we have thereby refuted the possibility of a special attitude. Other essential features such as empathy have been proposed. In addition, the possibility remains that this attitude is not distinguished by an essential property but rather by a set of features that identify aesthetic experience and, when analyzed from the vantage point of the aesthetic perceiver, constitute the aesthetic attitude. It is this latter alternative that I shall pursue here.

romantic aura. It has been given mythical and religious associations, likening the artist to the gods and his productive ability to the power of divine creation. It has been given irrational qualities by identifying artistic creation with anything from enraptured inspiration to mad frenzy. It has been the object of blind veneration and an element in hero worship. Reactions such as these simply make it more difficult to say anything intelligible and intelligent about the production of art.

On the other hand, the psychology of the artist, important as it may be for psychological research, has only a partial bearing on an understanding of the aesthetic field. It is relevant insofar as the activity of making an art object is a dimension of aesthetic experience, as we have already discovered. But the psychological dynamics by which the artist comes to create, his motives, aptitudes, and the like, are more the province of the psychology of individual behavior than of aesthetics proper. For these have to do not with art or the aesthetic field *per se* but rather with human action in general.

Similarly with the techniques of artistic creation, these may involve the technology of art, the craft with which the artist works skillfully to fashion an object. Or they may concern the mechanisms he uses to initiate his creative activity. The first belongs to the history of art, while the second is for the most part a matter for individual psychology. Certainly such lines are hard to draw. Yet it is clear in any case that the psychology of art has an intimate connection in many and varied ways with the experience of art and thus with the analysis of the aesthetic field. And it is this association that becomes the criterion of the relevance and significance of particular psychological investigations for the philosophy of art.

Material and Technological Factors

While their role may seem obvious, the influence of material and technological factors is often entirely overlooked. Yet they exert a profound effect on the kinds of art that people produce and on the qualitative experience of the aesthetic situation. The range of available materials and techniques with which an artist can work limits the possibility of the kinds of objects he can fashion, of the perceptual opportunities he will seize upon, and consequently of the experiential qualities in the aesthetic field. Whether an artist works in mosaic, in tempera, or on cave walls; whether he uses marble, concrete, or machine parts; whether he scores for aulos, sitar, harpsichord, piano, or tape recorder—all result in large measure from the extra-aesthetic conditions of the material resources of art at a particular time or place and from the kind and level of technological development of the artist's society. To be sure, the artist can always go back to materials and techniques of the past, but rarely does he restrict himself to these alone. Yet he can never transcend the technical limitations of his own age or materials. The wings of song must still conform to the laws of aerodynamics.

Thus an account of the aesthetic field in any particular case must pay close regard to the determining materials and technological influences. While the history of the arts has often been aware of these factors, it is uncommon for them to receive adequate attention when it comes to the analysis and criticism of specific art works. Here is the kind of contribution that responsible, informative scholarship and criticism can make. Instead of indulging in a display of erudition, of conceptual association, or of aesthetic speculation, the commentator can make an invaluable contribution by paying closer attention to the effects that the choice of particular materials and the selection of specific methods of working produce on aesthetic experience. How, for instance, do the peculiar features and limitations of oils or watercolors affect what the artist does and how he does it? How have mechanical devices that increase the speed of set changes in theatre affected dramatic action? How has the introduction of welding techniques influenced metal sculpture? How has straightening the curved bow of the Baroque violin expanded the technical resources of performance while eliminating older techniques such as playing simultaneously on more than two strings? By giving sensitive attention to such factors as these, artistic commentary can increase our awareness of art significantly. The origin and dependence of art on material, cultural, and human conditions thus determines the range of our changing experiences of art.

Historical Factors

Since the nineteenth century, scholarship in the arts has dealt with the historical development of the individual arts, with the significant events in the evolution of the arts, often trying to discover a pattern in their occurrence. As we have already seen, this kind of scholarship is directed largely to the history of art objects and of performance styles through which they are presented. Certainly our awareness of influential conditions and people, schools and movements, can help us in becoming attuned to the stylistic, technical, and aesthetic features of individual art objects. Yet this suggests another sense in which historical factors bear on the aesthetic field, and that is the ways in which historical elements influence aesthetic perception. There are fashions in the appreciation of art just as there are styles in the art object. In fact our discussion of the aesthetic field has tried to point out their functional inter-dependence, for such stylistic changes in both perception and production are intimately related to each other within the historical development of aesthetic experience.

Along with documenting the development of aesthetic perception goes the study of those things that influence it. The prevalent religious, moral, and cultural ideas of an age, the current views and theories that men hold about art, the state of human knowledge at various times, the dominant world view—all these exert a profound effect on the ways in which men perceive art. Here in fact is where the history of aesthetic perception merges with the history of ideas as well as with social history and cultural anthropology.

A clear example of the development of aesthetic perception, one which itself reflects the deliberate use of ideas about human society and experience that is changing, is Bertolt Brecht's Alienation Effect. Brecht attempted to break away from the subjective art of the last century and a half by introducing into theatrical experience a perception of the implacable objective forces that underlie human history and action. To do this he developed the idea of the Alienation Effect, which formulated a different relation between a stage play and its audience. According to it, the audience should not be led to empathize emotionally with the action on the stage, but rather to penetrate to an awareness of the immutable historical forces that led to the action. Here is a case in which a radical change in theatrical style is the direct outgrowth of a changed perception of the pattern and mode of human experience. Moreover, it is not a belief peculiar to Brecht, for other artists influenced by the materialist conception of history and social change attempt in various ways to achieve the same qualitative end.

The history of the arts and the history of taste, then, must be broadened to encompass the full range of aesthetic perception, thus becoming a history of aesthetic experience. Such a study would have considerable value, and not only for understanding particular art objects. The changing experience of art can also give us insights into the qualitative experiences of human life. To the extent that art is a social activity that reflects the qualitative perceptions of human experience in different times and places, the history of aesthetic experience can provide us with a singular opportunity to share the worlds of men in past and distant cultures.

Social and Cultural Factors

Because the experience of art is not set off from the full range of human experience by being exclusively personal, subjective, or otherwise private and inaccessible, it is, like all experience, greatly affected by sociocultural factors. This means that culture and society influence the things we perceive and the objects we create for perception. It also means that there are similar influences on the manner in which we each interpret such experience. A major instance of this is the prevalence of surrogate theories of art, which are the direct result of the popularity in western culture of nonaesthetic, particularly intellectual, models of perception.

There is, consequently, no pure perception. Things are perceived by people whose experience has conditioned them to adopt certain attitudes, to have particular expectations, and to be ready to respond in some ways and not in others. Even the phenomenological *epoché*, a technique designed to free perception from any presumption of existence by the suspension of judgment, is only partially successful. Edmund Husserl, the German philosopher who originated the *epoché,* went far beyond the purely perceptual by using it to achieve essential intuitions or essences. His conclusions may be explained at least in part by the Platonic predilection for universals of a man who made original contributions to the philosophy of mathematics. Such influences on perception that is intended to be uncommitted are well known and have been amply documented, yet the bearing this has on aesthetic perception is often overlooked.

For aesthetic experience is not the experience of an isolated individual; even when it occurs in seclusion, the percipient brings his culture with him. Most commonly, though, aesthetic experience occurs in the company of other people through the mediation of social institutions—in the setting of a concert hall, theatre, and art gallery—and this fact is not merely incidental. Even literary experience, which would seem to be most privately enjoyed, employs language, a social product, as its medium, and resembles the social act of communication more directly than other art.

Social and cultural factors comprise a vast array of profound influences on human, and consequently on aesthetic, experience. There is the effect of the structure, forms, and relationships of society on the kind of art that is produced. The comedies of manners of Molière, Congreve, Sheridan, and Wilde, for example, take their materials, including their highly cultivated characters and their witty conversation, from the salient features of the societies they lived in and wrote about. So, too, do the satires of Swift, Rabelais, and Cervantes; allegories like the medieval mystery plays and the Divine Comedy; genre paintings by Pieter Brueghel the Elder and the seventeenth century Dutch such as Vermeer and de Hooch. All draw on the objects, practices, and beliefs of their native cultures. And it is no coincidence that there are innumerable instances from painting and literature which derive from and work directly on social material.

Yet society influences art in ways that are often less obvious but all the more pervasive. Social traditions, ideological influences, religious beliefs, moral values—knowledge of these and other factors is necessary to illuminate the art of the novel, of the socialist painter, of Renaissance ecclesiastical music, of Victorian poetry. Commercial practices and economic conditions affect the kinds of musical and theatrical productions that a society will support, and this has much to do with artistic trends —from large scale, massive productions to intimate chamber works, from amateur performers to professional virtuosi, from experimental works to tired warhorses.

Indeed, the sociocultural influence is inescapable wherever we turn in our environment. For both man and his surroundings, natural and social, are so mutually formative that to speak of either alone is to falsify by extrapolation. We can learn here from the ecologists who have come to use the term *ecosystem* to denote the system of interrelated wholes formed by the interacting systems of living organisms and physical factors in environments which modify each other in various ways. An instance of this is the way in which the type of forest that grows in a particular region depends partly on the regional soil and climate, and yet at the same time the presence of the forest leads to an alteration of the climate, and the kind of forest, hardwood, coniferous, etc. affects the type of soil. In much the same way we can speak of the human ecosystem in which men are responsible for the concepts of their cultures, and at the same time cultural concepts and forces work on men to shape people in their own image.[34] Moreover, there is no way of separating man's cultural concepts from the conditions that surround him in his physical environment. The very same reciprocal influence works here, too. Prodded by desires for power, profit, fame, or satisfaction, man transfigures his landscape, alters his climate, causes social dislocations and transforms the entire fabric of his culture, all of which are reflected in the motives, materials, and subjectmatter of the arts. How then can they be ignored without blinding ourselves to qualities integral to the aesthetic vision?[35]

---

[34] Cf. Marston Bates, "A Naturalist at Large," *Natural History*, LXXVI, 6 (June-July 1967), 8-16.

[35] In spite of his own special perspective, D. H. Lawrence captured this point well:

The business of art is to reveal the relation between man and his

THE AESTHETIC TRANSACTION

We come finally to the core of this analysis, the experiential dynamic relationship in which all these elements and factors come together. Much of what I have cited here is obvious or well known. Much of the pertinent information is only tentative or problematical. Yet the influence on aesthetic experience of these and other such factors is undeniable, and so, therefore, is the role they play in understanding and explaining the aesthetic field.

We have come to see how the various elements in the aesthetic field work together in creative interplay. There is the art object, an intentional object that is aesthetically significant when there is an appropriate transaction which engages a perceiver with it. The art object provides the aesthetic situation with a strong source of stability, for its features are relatively constant despite differences in the perceiver's responses. The perceiver, on the other hand, brings certain stable features into the situation through his biological, social, and psychological similarities with other human beings. Yet he also introduces a wide degree of variability, graduating from cultural differences in response to those that result from individual differences in training and experience, physical endowment, attitude, and similar factors as they happen to function at a particular time and in a particular situation. Similar differences in the artist and in the performer introduce further variables into the aesthetic field. Moreover, the larger form of the field, indeed its very identifying traits, are shaped and directed by the wide range of cultural and physical factors that constitute the larger aesthetic environment. It is differences in these variable factors that account for differences in aesthetic response and judgment. Yet in spite of such variability, it remains possible to offer a unified analysis of aesthetic experience and to develop a genuine logic of aesthetic judgment.

This description of the aesthetic field, however, must be

---

circumambient universe, at the living moment. . . . It is a revelation of the perfected relation . . . for mankind. . . . The novel is the highest example of subtle interrelatedness that man has discovered.
"Morality and the Novel," in *Phoenix, The Posthumous Papers of D. H. Lawrence,* ed. by Edward D. McDonald (New York, Viking, 1936), p. 527.

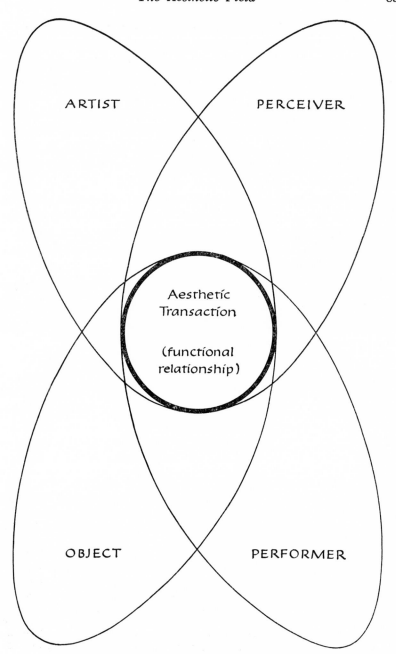

FIGURE 3.   The Aesthetic Transaction.

seen as an analytic account of what occurs in the experiential unity of the aesthetic situation. When we consider the field experientially rather than analytically, we can call it the aesthetic transaction (see Fig. 3).[36] The aesthetic field thus constitutes an attempt to analyze the structure of aesthetic experience. It is not the actual event but the product of an effort to cognize that event. All such attempts must, however, be sensitive to the experience of art, and thus they are always derivative. It might well be taken as a maxim that in aesthetics nothing works on principle.

This transactional experience involving an artistic perceiver and a perceptual aesthetic object is, then, quite literally the crux of the aesthetic field. Yet if you shake the field up, so to speak, everything becomes diffused into the same color. This is the perceptual integrity of aesthetic experience, whose characteristics must still be examined. Thus we turn from an analysis of the structure of the aesthetic field to an analysis of the features that make up aesthetic experience.

---

[36] Various features of this general position have been ably set forth by a number of recent writers. Cf. Louis Arnaud Reid, "Feeling and Expression in the Arts," *Journal of Aesthetics and Art Criticism*, XXV, 2 (Winter 1966), 123-135. Reid ends by stating his conviction that "the surface and the feeling import (analytically distinguishable) are in experience indivisibly one, and change together," and suggests that this may be "an illuminating key-idea for a systematic theory of aesthetics, and a better one than any known alternative hypothesis" (p. 134). Cf. also Matthew Lipman (*What Happens in Art*, New York, Appleton-Century-Crofts, 1967), who cites with approval the Gestalt psychologists who assign expressive qualities to perceptual objects. Lipman calls attention to Koffka's valuable distinction between the phenomenal whole and the physical thing, and notes the observation of Gestalt psychologists that "for the civilized adult, it is only in aesthetic experience that the close association between the external object and himself is restored" (p. 31).

IV

AESTHETIC EXPERIENCE

Everything for man is experience. This is not a metaphysical postulate; it is a tautology. As men are sentient and conscious, vital and responsive, they are experiencing. Experience is the general condition of human life.

How to describe human experience? How to identify its characteristic types? The answers to these questions cannot be prejudged, for experience assumes many modes. We cannot take the differentiation of experience into distinguishable kinds as something already given. It is rather a task for us to accomplish, a task in which we ought never to lose sight of the underlying continuity of human experience. The mystic and the scientist, the rationalist and the sensualist, the introspectionist and the businessman, the worshipper, the scholar, and the artist all devote themselves to different regions on the broad expanse of experience through the characteristic activities they pursue. Part of the task of understanding man's experience, then, lies in determining the functional features that identify and distinguish each particular mode from the others. Seldom is this done consciously and deliberately, but it is what we must attempt for aesthetic experience if we are to be at all successful in developing a firm grounding for aesthetic theory.

Since both the source and fulfillment of all art lie in human experience, it is perhaps the most important task of aesthetics to clarify the nature of the experience of art. The function of philosophy in relation to art here is no different from the philosophic function in any other region of human concern— to identify, describe, define, clarify, order, explain, in short, to work in conjunction with the other cognitive disciplines to try and explore and render understandable the various regions of human interest and activity. Thus the philosophic activity emerges out of our dealings in the world and returns to strengthen and enlarge them. This is as true with art as with anything else.

There is nothing new in seeing experience as the axis around which all other questions in aesthetics must rotate. Recent philological studies have tended to show that the Greek notion of *mimesis* signified not simple imitation but the activity of artistic creation.[1] Instead of being restricted to artistic objects and the resemblance they carry to the way things appear outside of art, mimesis connotes a particular kind of creative activity in which not the things that lie outside art but the objects in imitation are themselves the subject matter. By viewing mimesis as a creative activity, the classical imitation theories express, then, one version of experience as central in art. So, too, does the long history of identifying art with emotion. We see it in Plato's contention that poetry is the vehicle for communicating the divine inspiration of the poet through the rhapsode to the audience, and that the process possesses emotional intensity.[2] Aristotle, too, combines the use of imitation with the catharsis of pity and fear, and emotion informs both of these. And as is well known, emotional experience predominates in modern aesthetic thought. It becomes the foundation of Véron's theory of art as the expression of the artist's emotion and of Tolstoy's social view of art as communicating emotion. Even the formalists, who direct themselves primarily to the examination of art objects, discover in the "aesthetic emotion" the criterion for the success of an art object. Art is explained as dealing with feeling, from Ducasse's identification of art with pleasurable feeling to Langer's extension of feeling to encompass the whole range of man's sentience. And finally, experience is the central element in the aesthetics of Santayana and Dewey, and in those theories of art that identify a special kind of aesthetic experience, such as empathy or synaesthesis.

---

[1] Cf. Göran Sörbom, *Mimesis and Art, Studies in the Origin and Early Development of an Aesthetic Vocabulary* (Stockholm, Svenska Bokforlaget, 1968). Cf. also my review of this book, "From the Past of Aesthetics to Its Future," in *ETC.: A Review of General Semantics*, forthcoming.

[2] Cf. *Ion*, 533d-535c.

Thus the place of experience in an account of art has long been recognized, and the preceding chapters have attempted to make a case for the theoretical necessity of making it the central term. What is needed, however, is to become clearer about the kind of experience that is involved with art and about the ways in which it functions. What I shall attempt in this chapter is to develop an hypothesis about aesthetic experience that is empirically grounded and which thus possesses the unusual virtue of being verifiable, rather than resting on a tangled web of philosophical assumptions, concepts, and theory.

THE AESTHETIC MODE OF EXPERIENCE

The sole significance of all art lies in the experience which it engages. In speaking of a mode of experience that is characteristically aesthetic, I am not suggesting that experience is disjunctive, broken up into many irreconcilable forms. On the contrary, a careful description of the full range and variety of human experience must recognize the underlying continuity of its various types. Experiences associated with art are not radically different or sharply separated from other sorts of experiences. Depending upon the form, style, and period of art, aesthetic experience may verge on religious, mystical, scholarly, practical, athletic—indeed, on virtually every identifiable mode of experience. Furthermore, an aesthetic quality may be present in kinds of experiences predominantly different from it.

Thus while aesthetic experience has an identity, it is not set off from other modes of experience by some unique attribute. Indeed, the aesthetic is not a separate *kind* of experience but rather a *mode* in which experience may occur. For this reason I shall not speak of "*the* aesthetic experience" but rather of "aesthetic experience," experience qualified by the presence of characteristics which make it aesthetic. Instead of being sharply demarcated by possessing some special, unique feature, it is continuous with the whole range of human activity.

To speak more technically, the modes of experience are not ontological; they are rather empirically determined patterns that have histories and that are eminently mutable. By using the term "aesthetic experience" rather than "*the* aesthetic experience," I am deliberately attempting to see the aesthetic qualitatively rather than substantively, and to avoid the implication that the aesthetic mode of experience is set apart from other modes. It is more a perspective or *phase* of experience than a *kind* of experience.[3]

In attempting to characterize aesthetic experience, it will be useful to adopt what we might call a matrix theory of definition. Rather than seeking in Aristotelian fashion the one essential attribute of the aesthetic mode of experience, we must rather determine the set of coordinates that commonly appear together and are the basis on which we recognize and distinguish this mode of experience from others. Not only must we enumerate the relevant factors; we must also determine their relative emphasis and interrelationships.[4] This is itself an empirical inquiry, to be pursued not by stipulating what these features

---

[3] One recent writer has advanced the suggestive proposal that rather than a philosophy of experience which is "multiform" by demarcating experience into distinct modes, a philosophy of experience ought rather to be "multiphase" by seeing a common underlying resemblance in all experience, characterized at various times by different dominant features. In the case of aesthetics, an adjectival analysis which distinguishes experience in its aesthetic aspect from other aspects of experience is preferable to a substantival analysis which distinguishes aesthetic experience from other distinct types of experience. This makes explicit the continuity between experience that is aesthetic and experience that is predominantly something else. One may add to this the further proposal that a substantival analysis be foregone entirely in favor of a verbal and adverbial one, in which the general activity of "experiencing" is seen to assume a variety of forms with different dominant characteristics. Cf. P. Romanell, "Prolegomena to Any Naturalistic Aesthetics," *J. of Aesthetics and Art Criticism*, XIX, 142; also J. H. Randall, Jr., *Nature and Historical Experience* (New York, 1958), p. 286, who also proposes an adverbial analysis.

[4] While this includes the main features of the Aristotelian definition by genus and differentia, it is more comprehensive, and does not entail a prior commitment to any ontology of essence and accident. D. H. Parker has made a similar proposal for the definition of art. He argued that this cannot be done by discovering a single common characteristic that all art possesses. We must rather seek a complex set of characteristics. He, himself, proposed a voluntaristic theory in which art is '. . . the provision of satisfaction (of wishes and desires) through the imagination, social significance, and harmony." Cf. "The Nature of Art," in E. Vivas and M. Krieger, eds., *The Problems of Aesthetics* (New York, 1953), p. 90.

are, but rather by discerning the syndrome that is characteristic of aesthetic experience within the broad range of human activity, observation, and testimony. We cannot begin, therefore, by stating *a priori* criteria by which aesthetic experience may be recognized. We must rather start by examining and describing the experience people generally associate with the various forms of fine art and with the aesthetic perception of nature.[5]

This is really not a proposal for something new. In the literature of aesthetics, the experience of art has often preceded its theoretical definition. A critic or aesthetician has in mind certain forms or styles of artistic production on the basis of which he sets up his categories and defines his terms and criteria. Ortega favors modern art of the early twentieth century in which only a tenuous connection with representational features is retained. Bell and Fry champion fully nonrepresentational painting; the expression theorists, romantic art; the imitation theorists, representational painting and realism and naturalism in literature. These and others implicitly use what is for them fresh and genuine art as the standard by which to clarify aesthetic experience and to judge works of art. By consciously turning to those experiences we commonly regard as aesthetic, then, we are not begging the question of what art is. We are rather beginning the quest for an answer by affirming that the answer to that question depends on the experience of art. It is a question that is "empiriogenic," to use a term that Marvin Farber has proposed, a question that originates in the conditions of human experience.

---

[5] Stephen Pepper makes a similar proposal when he advises that we seek the norm of aesthetic beauty in the classics, since they provide "the safest well recognized group of facts for roughly locating in a preliminary way the field of our inquiry." *Aesthetic Quality* (New York, 1937, 1938), p. 15. Pepper's suggestion is basically sound, although it is limited for two reasons. First, Pepper locates the field of inquiry in objects rather than experience, thus confining himself to a single group of aesthetic facts. Second, he shuts out data that challenge traditional aesthetics by not including the contemporary arts, even though their aesthetic status and artistic stature are often controversial. The arts of the evermoving present are the leading edge of aesthetic sensibility, and it is this which it is the task of aesthetic theory to explain. Never has this been more true than in the third quarter of the twentieth century when the range of objects and experiences has been greatly enlarged and transformed.

Like the other problems of aesthetic theory, this must be approached, not by prescription or postulate, but inductively by explicit recourse to the relevant experiences of men.[6]

CHARACTERISTICS OF AESTHETIC EXPERIENCE

What set of features, then, can be taken as defining that phase in the continuity of experience that is aesthetic? Clearly a disclaimer is in order here, for any such matrix definition can only be hypothetical, tested and refined by the degree of its success in giving an accurate and comprehensive account of our aesthetic involvement. There is no infallible basis on which to claim that an account is authentic. One can do no more here than try to examine experience that is by general agreement predominantly aesthetic, consciously expunging the influence—moral, religious, pedagogical, metaphysical, historical, and cultural—of any *a priori* expectations of what that experience must be like.

Here the statements of creative artists are often informative, especially when the artists do not bring to their descriptions aesthetic or metaphysical preconceptions but rather attempt to explain as simply and directly as they can what it is they do, think, and feel in and about artistic creation. The responses of sensitive observers who are free from preconceived notions of what they will find are often informative, and so too are studies in child psychology. Undoubtedly the most important pre-requisite is a receptivity to what actually transpires in our encounter with the arts and not to what one thinks should occur or wants to occur. In no area of experience is such description more difficult.

What is offered, here, therefore, makes no pretense of being a final account; it is rather a hypothetical one which will be verified by the extent to which it reveals aspects of the experience of art which were overlooked, unexplained, misinterpreted,

---

[6] See the discussion of this point in Chapter I. The question is also treated in A. Berleant, "A Note on the Problem of Defining 'Art,'" *Philosophy and Phenomenological Research*, XXV, 2 (December, 1964), 239-241. Reprinted in H. G. Duffield, ed., *Problems in Criticism of the Arts* (San Francisco, Chandler, 1968), pp. 240-242.

or rejected as inadmissible, thus enlarging and deepening the quality and extent of that experience.

Active-Receptive

As biological factors influence the aesthetic field, so too, does the aesthetic mode of experience have a biological aspect. With the disappearance of distance comes an involvement, a participation, a contribution that is part of our experience of art. Just as the creature in a natural environment engages in a complex interplay of action and reaction, performing upon his surroundings and responding and adapting to them at the same time, so the experience of art, as natural experience, calls forth similar behavior.

In the aesthetic field there is a basic similarity in the roles of the artist and the perceiver, the artistic and the aesthetic, and this same harmony of action and reaction is shared by the experiential dimension of the field. Picasso, among many, testifies to the activity of artist and perceiver when he observes,

> The picture is not thought out and determined beforehand; rather while it is being made it follows the mobility of thought. Finished, it changes further, according to the condition of him who looks at it. A picture lives its life like a living creature, undergoing the changes that daily life imposes upon us. That is natural, since a picture lives only through him who looks at it.[7]

Nor is the active involvement of the spectator a recent development. The canvases of Tintoretto, to cite one case, create movement with such effectiveness that the pictorial space tends to appear as a continuation of the space in which the observer is standing, thus drawing him into the events depicted in the painting. "In extreme instances Tintoretto may be said to blast his way into our sensibilities."[8]

Indeed, the involvement of the perceiver is a factor in the experience of all the visual arts. In different ways one is a participating part of the space of the object and of the space within which the object is encountered. We live in architectural

---

[7] In B. Ghiselin, ed., *The Creative Process* (New York, 1955), p. 57.

[8] John Ives Sewall, *A History of Western Art* (New York, Holt, 1953), p. 768.

space, move as an equal object in urban space, in sculptural space, and among paintings on exhibit. In perceiving pictorial space, we become to that extent a part of it, and as perceptual participants we move, so to speak, within it. In much the same way, time is an experienced element in art, a factor in our response and through which we move and engage objects in the aesthetic field. Empathy theorists like Lipps and Lee have stressed somatic participation in aesthetic perception. They have observed how muscular movements are an integral part of aesthetic experience in such a way that there is an emulative physical participation in the aesthetic response. In our physical positions, postures, and movements, we join with an art object in a common activity.[9] Mass, for instance, possesses a presence of its own into which we enter directly. We experience a physical imbalance in our bodies when we encounter a sculpture that has formal imbalance. And in music, our subvocal participation is sometimes distressingly obvious when we strain with a singer reaching for a high note. What is consciously apparent under stress is but an exaggeration of a physical involvement that is always present.

In dance the importance of the active ingredient in the experience of art is perhaps most immediately apparent. Dance critics, for example, agree in maintaining that the audience at a dance performance must not be passive but must actively respond, otherwise "only half a performance has taken place."[10] Active involvement is literally an essential part of the appreciative experience of dance. John Martin observes that

> . . . though to all outward appearances we shall be sitting quietly in our chairs, we shall nevertheless be dancing synthetically with all our musculature. . . . It is the dancer who functions to lead us into imitating his actions with our faculty for inner mimicry in order that we may experience his feelings. Facts he could tell us, but feelings he cannot convey in any other way than by arousing them in us through sympathetic action.[11]

------

[9] See Vernon Lee, "Empathy," and Theodor Lipps, "Empathy, Inner Imitation, and Sense-Feelings," in M. Rader, ed., *A Modern Book of Esthetics*, 3rd ed. (New York, Holt, Rinehart & Winston, 1960), pp. 370-374 and 374-382.

[10] Walter Terry, *Ballet, A New Guide to the Liveliest Art* (New York, Dell Publ., 1959), p. 24.

[11] John Martin, *Introduction to the Dance* (New York, Norton, 1939), p. 10.

And Walter Terry explains why:

> For if we respond kinesthetically to a dance movement, we take part in the performance of dance itself and by taking part, we know more perfectly what each movement means—whether that meaning is literal, symbolic, fantastic, romantic, or virtuosic, or purely kinetic—and why each such movement was created by the choreographer.[12]

The experience of other arts reveals the same kind of active, responsive receptivity. Even literature, which may appear at first to be the most cerebral and sedentary of the arts, calls for the reader's help. Notice how the effectiveness of literature will vary by the extent to which the reader's work is done for him. Some literature tells us everything down to the last detail. Everything is complete, everything is obvious, everything is predictable. The author supplies us with our interpretations and judgments, and all we need do is identify the words. In this description we recognize, perhaps, the pulp magazine. At the other extreme, effective literature is uninterpreted. Everything is not given. Instead it draws the reader into the experience being recounted.[13] Working imaginatively, the reader colors in the outlines, drawing upon his personal and cultural autobiography to supply the concrete content. In this way he participates in the creation of the experience that is that art work, and in this way the object becomes, ironically, more real, more alive, and more significant. At times the very simplicity of the tale allows it to function as a universal that is particularized in the individual imagination. The novels of Ernest Hemingway and Alan Paton and the stories of Isak Dinesen often possess this mythic quality. The essential place that imagination has in literature shows how basic the reader's contribution is to the literary experience. The reader must, in effect, give content to the literary variables which appear in the unavoidable abstractions of language.

Qualitative

Like every mode of experience, aesthetic experience has essential unity. Hence it is difficult to talk about any one of

---

[12] Terry, *op. cit.*, p. 11.

[13] Cf. S. I. Hayakawa, *Language in Thought and Action*, 2nd ed. (New York, Harcourt, Brace & World, 1963, 1964), pp. 128-130.

its characteristics without having the others insinuate themselves into the discussion. For we are not identifying elements that combine to make the experience of art distinctive. Rather we are attempting to translate into discursive thought the undulating iridescence of an integral experience. This is perhaps especially the case with the qualitativeness of aesthetic experience.

While we may speak of a situation or an idea, it is more usual to take quality to refer to the sensory features of experience. Before primary experience is cognized by being categorized, quantified, conceptually ordered and manipulated in some way, it is filled with the sensory qualities of the world. Colors, sounds, movements, masses, lines, kinesthetic and tactile sensations that are rough, smooth, sticky, warm, dry, wet, chilly—all these crowd experience in endless, confusing, and disordered variety. Like Kant's percepts, the qualitative aspect of experience, prior to the ordering activity of reflective intelligence, is cognitively blind. Contrary to Kant, however, the conceptual process is not contemporaneous with sensory experience but proceeds beyond pure sensation from the attempt to carry on and control activity effectively.

Self-sufficiency, a perfection of sensation, is the most salient feature of pure experience. It rests on the active involvement of men in the experiential situation. For this is gross, uncomprehended experience that antecedes the distinctions of intellect. The awareness of identity and of the limits of the self, manipulation of objects, and telic arrangement of activities, all have no place in experience that is predominately qualitative.

Experience in its qualitative dimension plays a special and indeed a major role in aesthetic perception. S. C. Pepper has shown how the aesthetic character of a situation can be defined by reference to the intuition of quality, and how its value can be appraised in the light of the extensiveness and richness of its quality.[14] Many have noted how aesthetic experience invokes complete sensory involvement. Bernard Berenson has called attention to the effects that aesthetic perception has on the

---

[14] *The Basis of Criticism in the Arts* (Cambridge, Mass., Harvard U. Press, 1963), pp. 56-58.

vaso-motor system, and has spoken of art as "ideated sensation."[15] John Dewey has contrasted the qualitative, physical character of aesthetic experience with language and its intellectual effect. For him, space and time, for example, are essentially qualitative in experience.[16] Still others have commented upon the primacy of perception in experience and the influence this has had on metaphorical expressions in language.[17]

The qualitativeness of aesthetic experience has come in for special recognition in the modern arts. This is clearly the case with impressionistic music and painting, with abstract expressionism in painting, and with the serial music of Webern. Moreover, one of the most salient features of the contemporary arts is their tendency to exploit the immediate force of sensory qualities. In the environmental arts such as happenings, environments, city planning, films, light shows, and mixed media, the qualitative nature of the experience of art has been identified with its intuitive sensuousness through direct involvement in the immediacy of pure experience. As characteristically qualitative and perceptual in nature, then, aesthetic experience is in direct contrast with experiences which forego the sensuousness of experience to emphasize what is quantitative, conceptual, and abstract.

Much of what we can point out in describing aesthetic experience follows from its qualitative character. For to speak of our experience of art as qualitative is to regard it as sensuous, as immediate, unique, noncognitive, intrinsic, and situational. Yet it remains for us to see in just what ways these various aspects of quality function in our encounter with art and reveal its perceptual richness.

Sensuous

The sensory features of aesthetic experience have, as we have seen, a special and distinctive place in the qualitative

---

[15] *The Italian Painters of the Renaissance* (The Clarendon Press, 1930), p. 198; Cf. Virgil C. Aldrich, *Philosophy of Art* (Englewood Cliffs, N. J., Prentice-Hall, 1963), p. 18.

[16] *Art as Experience* (New York, Minton, Balch & Co., 1934), pp. 206ff., 214-216f.

[17] Cf. James Edie, "Expression and Metaphor," *Phil. and Phen. Res.*, XXIII, 4 (June 1963), pp. 538-40, 543, 560-1.

dimension of experience. Moreover, these qualities often assume
an intensity and concentration that emphasizes their sensuousness.
At times, the sensuousness of aesthetic perception may enlarge
and extend itself so that it merges with the overtly sensual.
It is important for this discussion to see how sensuous experience
can be freed of inhibiting restrictions and allowed to fill the
space of perception as fully as it will.

Although it might be possible to speak of pleasure in this
connection, I have not done so. To discuss art in terms of
pleasure would be to introduce unnecessary confusions and
complications. Pleasure, for example, has often been regarded
with suspicion by many writers on aesthetics. Even when its
presence is admitted, some philosophers feel an overpowering
need to remove pleasure from the place of natural experience
in order to prevent it from becoming sullied with the grossness
of a sensuous response. Kant is one instance of this. While he
defined the judgment of taste as concerned with pleasure, it was
pleasure that is disinterested, universal, unintellectual, and what
is most to the point here, different from the pleasures of sense
or of ordinary emotions. Such an account attenuates pleasure
to the point where it becomes unrecognizable.

There are many reasons which underlie the reluctance to
identify sensory pleasures with the pleasures of art. One set
of objections is clearly moralistic, and associates sensory pleasure
with titillation. Yet to naturalize the pleasure of the arts hardly
requires us to view them as passive and nugatory. Aesthetic
pleasure is not the feeble delight of one so ennervated as merely
capable of being titillated by art, but of one who contributes
his organic vitality as part of his full response. We must, in fact,
include the vital pleasure of the body as an actively sensing
instrument as a dimension of our full participation with the arts.
Rather, though, than speak of pleasure and inherit the history
of controversy and confusion that has accompanied the notion,
it will better serve a clear and accurate description of aesthetic
experience to explore it in terms of its sensuous dimension.

It is, in fact, its very sensuous concreteness and immediacy
that makes the aesthetic the most naturalistic of all experiences.
At no time do we come as close to the vital fusion of sense,

imagination, environment, and intense awareness than when we are participating successfully in the experience of art. Indeed, this sensuous concreteness is one source of the power of the arts on social and political issues. Nowhere do we feel injustice more acutely, grasp the sweep of history more completely, share the scope of human aspirations and human despair more profoundly than we do through our experience of the arts.[18]

Those objections to the sensuousness of the arts that may be most persistent of all are directed against associating aesthetic experience with the sensual. There is a long history of suspicion toward the arts on this account. Only reluctantly has a place in aesthetic experience been accorded the senses, and then only with distinctions and restrictions, such as between the higher and lower senses, the aesthetic and nonaesthetic senses, and the sensuous and the sensual.[19] From Greek philosophy to the present, philosophers have regarded sight and hearing alone as aesthetic senses. These are distance receptors and suited the classical aesthetic which prevailed well into the eighteenth century. This view took aesthetic theory to be concerned with the nature of beautiful object, to the effective exclusion of the percipient, who was allowed to involve himself only disinterestedly and at a distance. The contact receptors such as touch and taste, on the other hand, have been regarded as nonaesthetic. They prevent us from assuming proper distance from art, since they are sullied with the practical exchanges that take place among men and things.[20]

By isolating the senses from one another and discriminating among them, traditional aesthetics circumscribed the domain of aesthetic experience and confined it to those regions that were acceptable by social, moral, political, religious, and metaphysical

[18] Cf. George Lukacs: "All true works of art are, in the precise sense of the term, anti-theodicies." *Die Eigenart des Aesthetischen*, II, p. 837.

[19] A more extended discussion of these and related issues may be found in A. Berleant, "The Sensuous and the Sensual in Aesthetics," *Journal of Aesthetics and Art Criticism* (XXIII, 2, Winter 1964), 185-192; reprinted in *Philosophical Essays on Curriculum* (Ed.) R. Guttchen and B. Bandman (Philadelphia, Lippincott, 1969).

[20] Cf. D. H. Parker, *The Principles of Aesthetics*, 2nd ed. (New York, Appleton-Century-Crofts, 1946), p. 45f. for an illustration of the traditional view.

criteria. Only in recent decades have we begun to emancipate ourselves from such nonaesthetic restrictions. With the help of fresh thinking in philosophy and psychology, we have come to recognize the perceptual integration, the nondiscreteness, of the senses. Certain perceptual qualities like softness and brightness are multi-sensory, appearing to touch, taste, smell, sound, and sight. There is also the evidence of the synesthesias or intersensory effects, as when visual impressions accompany auditory stimuli. Some investigators, in fact, propose the view that the senses comprise a unity, one that is manifested in the unity of the modalities of sensation.[21] Dewey's observation may well be right, that "a particular sense is simply the outpost of a total organic activity in which all organs, including the functioning of the autonomic system, participate."[22]

Creative artists have often been aware of the integrated participation of the senses. The painter Hans Hofmann, who exercised so powerful an influence on contemporary art, includes hearing and touch, the sense of space and movement, in painting. ". . . (S)eeing with the physical eyes borders on blindness. We see, indeed, with all our senses. All our senses are dependent upon each other in their action upon the mind where they join and overlap."[23] And from another age and culture, the Japanese poet Matsuo Basho, who originated the genre of *haiku* and was one of its greatest masters, had a profound belief in the inter-relatedness of the five senses. An experience was something he perceived in its total force, odor, color, and sound being fused into one. Many of his poems give literary expression to synesthesia.[24] It is no surprise that the most intensely perceptual

---

[21] Werner and Straus take this position. Straus goes still farther and identifies an inner connection of sensing with vital living movement. Cf. Erwin Straus, *The Primary World of Senses* (London, Collier Macmillan, 1963), pp. 214-15 ff., 233-4. M. Lipman, *What Happens in Art* (New York, Appleton-Century-Crofts, 1967), pp. 28-34; A. Berleant, "The Sensuous and the Sensual in Aesthetics," pp. 186-188.

[22] *Art as Experience*, p. 218.

[23] Hans Hofmann, Exhibition Catalogue, Kootz Gallery, New York, January 1960.

[24] Mokoto Ueda, "Basho and the Poetics of Haiku," *Journal of Aesthetics and Art Criticism*, XXI, 4 (Summer, 1963), pp. 428-9.

styles of art recognize most clearly the perceptual fusion of the senses and their full and unified claim.

Despite a tradition of hostility toward the sensuous force of the arts, it has never been possible to suppress this phase of experience. And in the last century and a half as the arts have gradually emancipated themselves from conformity to non-aesthetic demands, the sensuous in our experience of art has asserted itself with greater freedom. Openness to the wide range and subtle variety of experience may be a prime source of the artistic impulse. Whatever its form or medium, its place or object, creative intelligence looks upon human experience as if for the first time. It is for this reason that the arts are always radical in the original sense of the term, leading us back to the source of every meaning in experience, testing its human authenticity and relevance, and constantly challenging the restrictions that custom or habit have imposed on us. Thus the arts pose a perpetual threat to convention and the established morality.[25]

It is remarkable to observe the intellectual contortions into which writers will twist themselves in the effort to avoid giving full scope to aesthetic sensuousness. Schelling is an exemplary instance of this. In his lectures on the philosophy of art (1802-5), Schelling replaced the sensuousness of music with spirituality. Music, he maintained, was the art "which to the greatest degree divests itself of corporeality and is borne upon invisible, almost spiritual wings." This led him to assert that true, ideal music is actually nonsensuous and, indeed, suprasensuous, and thus not heard at all![26] One encounters current writers who engage in similar intellectual gymnastics, such as denying the essential temporality of music in order to spatialize it and hence transform it into an object that can be distanced.[27] This has been carried to the extreme of regarding music as literally spatialized in the form of the phonograph record.

Instances of this mistrust of aesthetic sensuousness could be

---

[25] Cf. J. Dewey, *Art as Experience*, p. 189.

[26] Cf. Alfred Einstein, *Music in the Romantic Era* (New York, Norton, 1947), p. 340.

[27] Patricia Carpenter, "The Musical Object," *Current Musicology*, 5 (1967), pp. 65-9 and passim.

multiplied endlessly. One writer has observed that cultural or personal attitudes toward the body have influenced artistic techniques, such as perspective. Romanesque frescoes lacked perspective because it was believed that physical perception distorted things. Perception through the soul, on the other hand, was uncorrupted.[28] Another case of the same suspicion is the need of many writers to dissociate the beautiful from the (sexually) desirable.[29]

This last is probably the most deep-seated of all restraints on the full extension of aesthetic perception. Yet it is one of the directions in which the sensuous dimension of art has developed in recent times. A good deal of interest has been shown by the modern arts in exploiting their sensual possibilities, and at times they have embraced the overtly erotic. This is hardly a new development in art, but it has become a more freely expressive feature in the West during recent times than ever before.

Eros, however, is never happy nor fulfilled when it is localized, and the erotic impulse readily diffuses itself so that every part and every movement of the body arouses our fascinated attention. Increasingly we are allowing ourselves to recognize the central role that the human body plays in many of the arts. The beauty of bodily movement has relaxed from the formal loveliness of ballet into the freer flexings of modern dance. In contemporary dance, at times, literally sexual actions are simulated. The art of the mime, too, hinges upon the enormous range of expressive gestures of the body.[30] In the fine arts, the magnetic allure of the body has long held such fascination for artists that Kenneth Clark has called the nude not the subject of art but rather a form of art. Moreover, the desire for union with another human body has so powerful a place among our basic drives that the nude as an art form is one which cannot and should not suppress erotic feeling.[31] We are more ready now than ever

----

[28] M. Lipman, "The Aesthetic Presence of the Body," *Journal of Aesthetics and Art Criticism*, XV (1957), pp. 428-9.

[29] For one instance of this, see Clive Bell, *Art* (New York, Capricorn Books, 1958), p. 28.

[30] Cf. M. Lipman, "The Aesthetic Presence of the Body."

[31] K. Clark, *The Nude* (New York, Pantheon Books, 1956), pp. 4, 8.

before to recognize the legitimate place of the erotic in art and of art in the erotic. Few objects possess such intensity of emotional involvement as does the human body, and it is little wonder that artists constantly find themselves drawn to reveal its endless transformations and to write new variations on this fundamental theme.

The persistent rediscovery of the body as a subject or form of art has not been confined to its representations. As both the origin and the ideal of creative thought and action, the body becomes a source from which other essentially nonrepresentational arts draw. Architecture is one case of this. The most obvious use of the body in architecture is in sculptures and reliefs of the human figure to adorn temples and other structures. Especially salient examples are the tenth century Indian erotic temple sculptures, such as the façade of the Kandāriya Mahādeva temple, Khajurāho, erected by King Ganda Chandella in 1002. Here the forms of human sexuality are fused with religious philosophy and the demands of architectural engineering and space for human use.

Yet there are organic influences on both architectural structures and on their human uses and relations. One recent writer sees the mark of great architecture not in expression or symbolism but instead "in the sensuous impact of its space and mass."[32] Moreover, Geoffrey Scott, in his *The Architecture of Humanism,* conceives architecture as "an art of design based on the human body and its states." Convinced that architecture must, like the body, possess organic qualities, Vasari, in the sixteenth century, expressed a similar view when he praised a building that seemed "not built, but born." Michelangelo, too, insisted that one must master the human figure, especially its anatomy, to comprehend architecture. And in fact a recent writer, stressing the functional relation of architecture to human uses, describes the relation between men and the architectural container as symbiotic. Interestingly, he finds a uterine analogy most sug-

_____

[32] Albert Bush-Brown, "How a Building May Fail to Become Architecture," from "The Architectural Polemic," *Journal of Aesthetics and Art Criticism,* VIII (1959), p. 147.

gestive of the relation between man and his architectural environment.[33]

A full development of function in architecture and design so that it includes the qualities of human action and response leads to the important notion of organic functionalism. Not only do functionally successful buildings acquire the quality that organic objects have of so identifying themselves with their function that they come to symbolize it as well, as in the grasping uses and form of the hand or the stealthy appearance and tread of the feline. The same is true of machines, utensils, and buildings that function successfully, embodying in their forms the functions they perform. Contrast, for instance, the shape of a glider with that of a supersonic airliner, where the different aerodynamic forms reveal different uses. The one describes lightness, buoyancy, grace; the other power, thrust, and enormous speed. Similar qualities appear in the swooping cantilevered roof combined with the airiness of great expanses of glass that mark Saarinen's TWA terminal at Kennedy Airport, both made possible by techniques and materials of modern engineering. Acoustical demands are both resolved and embodied in the organic forms of Kleinhan's Music Hall in Buffalo, which is also by Saarinen.

Yet Mumford and others go beyond this to insist that functionally designed objects should not only reveal in their form the function they perform. They must in addition incorporate human needs and preferences as an integral part of the concept of organic functionalism. Mechanical function is not enough; the qualities that an architectural environment creates for human experience are an equal part of function. And what can be said of building can be said, *a fortiori*, of the functioning of a city.[34]

Less obvious, perhaps, but all the more suggestive, is the diffusion of the proportions of the body into objects that at first would not seem related. Certain societies, for example, give

---

[33] J. M. Fitch, "The Aesthetics of Function," *Annals of the New York Academy of Sciences*, Vol. 128, Article 2 (Sept. 27, 1965), pp. 709, 712.

[34] Lewis Mumford has done much to develop these ideas. Cf., for example, *Art and Technics* (New York, Columbia University Press, 1952), pp. 116, 127. See also A. Berleant, "Aesthetic Function," in *Phenomenology and Naturalism*, Dale Riepe (Ed.), forthcoming.

their musical instruments sexual connotations through their shape as well as their sound.[35] Moreover, one can discover an analogy with human proportions in the satisfying abstract forms of a pot or an architectural molding. Kenneth Clark, for instance, discerns a resemblance between Michelangelo's outline for a molding for the Laurenziana and the back of one of his atheletes in the Sistine.[36]

Shapes and forms everywhere suggest the pervasiveness of organic features. There is a correspondence between tangible patterns and their meaning or significance, what Gestalt psychologists call "isomorphism." Yet this may be more than a correspondence; it may indeed be an identity in perceptual experience that joins together these patterns and our feeling qualities. Sculptors often take special advantage of this, as we can see from the biomorphic forms of Arp, the sensuous nudes of Maillol and the sensual ones of Lachaise and Rodin (e.g. "The Kiss").

Moreover, the world around us reveals shapes with which our bodies vibrate in sympathetic harmony. The curved line and convex surface are organic forms, and when they appear in inanimate objects they nonetheless convey organic qualities. It is no coincidence that the rocker looks and feels more comfortable than the straight chair, although both may be made of the same maple. Even the vertical and the horizonal reflect bodily attitudes, the first being tense, active, requiring effort to keep a precarious balance, while the second is more stable and relaxed. Many objects, too, are designed and arranged so that they reflect the symmetry, basic divisions, and distribution of masses of the body. The table is a case in point. Not only does it almost always have legs (or possibly a pedestal) rather than being, for example, a cylinder set on end, perhaps with knee space hollowed out. But we also feel compelled to place something in the center of its surface such as a vase or a lamp. As we experience it, the world assumes a perceptual anthropomorphism (what Gestalt psychologists call physiognomic qualities), and this is all the more acute in art where our perception is at its most heightened.

----

[35] Cf. C. Sachs, *The Wellsprings of Music* (The Hague, 1962).

[36] *The Nude*, p. 348.

We have thus come full circle from our original discussion of the sensuous in aesthetic experience. The extension of its sensuous dimension leads us to cast aside moral and metaphysical inhibitions and accept the sensual and openly erotic. The erotic, moreover, infuses the entire human body with significance, and we extend this feeling import to the objects that surround us in the perceptual directness of primary experience, returning again to the sensuous qualities of perception.

Once we recognize how completely the sensuous has humanized the entire range of our perceptual experience, we can understand one of the reasons for the constant and enormous expansion of the range of art. During the past century and a half the locus of art has been transferred from the plane of what is rare and elevated to the level of the ordinary and commonplace. The advent of the realistic and naturalistic novel, the depiction of the tragedy of the ordinary man in contrast with that of the aristocrat, the choice in painting of the homely subject over the honored, and in contemporary art, the rise of pop art and our new and inclusive perception of the environment ranging from the ordinary to the vulgar, all this and more has opened our eyes to the sensuous qualities of the world around us, often with the added force of social criticism. Aesthetic sensuousness is not effete sensibility nurtured through withdrawal. On the contrary, it requires the full vitality of human responsiveness, and makes both our world more human and our humanity more worldly.

Immediate

One source of the intrinsic forcefulness and critical power of the arts lies in the immediacy that infuses our encounter with them. This does not mean that the experience of art is momentary; no experience that possesses the fullness, the rich significance of art can be confined to the passing instant. When we approach art in the context of the aesthetic field, we see that aesthetic experience has real breadth. Art recalls the traces of past experience, both aesthetic and nonaesthetic. For part of the richness and the unpredictability of art lies in its ability to tap the innermost recesses of memory, of vague recollection, and add the dimension of the past to what is most intensely present. Yet this past may reach beyond our personal history into a common wellspring of human life. Roger Fry wonders whether the emotional tone of pure beauty "does not get its force from arousing some very deep, very vague, and immensely generalized reminiscences." Art may reach down to the "substratum of all the emotional colors of life, to something which underlies all the particular and specialized emotions of actual life." Its emotional energy seems to originate in "the very conditions of our existence by its relation of an emotional significance in time and space."[37]

Consider the effect that familiarity plays in experiencing an art object. Often our most frequent encounters with art and probably our most successful ones occur when we reread a novel or poem, see a new performance of a favorite play, or hear a performance of a familiar musical composition. When the sequence of events, the succession of lines, the movement of sound is known and anticipated, we no longer rely on the suspense of the unknown, the excitement of discovery. These may not be artistic virtues. Newness may evoke curiosity, interest, even intrigue, yet it also carries with it confusion, oversights, and missed perceptions. As with people, an introduction merely initiates acquaintance; it takes further encounters for this to develop into friendship. (If we tire of people as we tire of art, is this not a comment on the ineffectiveness of our relationship?) The richness of an art object, and hence its cumulative value, emerges from its functional success.

Singular art, art of which there is but one appearance or performance, introduces a complication. Moving patterns of colored light all possess a close resemblance through the similarity of their medium. While the patterns constantly vary, movement becomes central, and the types of shapes and the ways in which the patterns change constantly recur. It is clearly with the materials that we achieve familiarity. Yet even here, formal principles of construction may be used, with the only

---

[37] Roger Fry, "The Artist and Psychoanalysis," from *The Hogarth Essays.* Reprinted in M. Rader, ed., *A Modern Book of Esthetics,* 3rd ed. (New York, Holt, Rinehart, and Winston, 1960), p. 309.

difference being the new medium of light. Thomas Wilfred's
Lumia Suite, op. 158, for example, receives its structural inspiration from music. Happenings are another instance of singular
art, since most Happenings are unique occurrences, not intended
to be repeated. Still, the situations that Happenings develop
stress the use of familiar objects and everyday occurrences,
although these are dislocated by being placed in a new context,
and the scripts are generally quite simple. Moreover, since
Happenings take the continuity between art and life as a central
premise, they make their own case for familiarity.

Yet what is striking about the experience of art is how it
leads the many springs of experience into a common stream in
the ever-moving present. Art evokes present effects of a great
backlog of living; it sets up sympathetic vibrations of feeling,
thought, and body. Perhaps this temporal aspect can best be
described metaphorically by comparing aesthetic experience to
the concentric ripples made by a leaf settling on the surface of
still water. Its impact is strongest at the point of contact, but
it moves outward wider and softer. To regard the experience
of art as a momentary pulsation of ecstasy, as Pater does in his
Conclusion to *The Renaissance*,[38] is to assume the confining
posture of the esthete. It is to be blind, not only to the spreading
wavelets, but to the tree and pond as well—necessary conditions
for receptivity.

This process of reactivating the past demands the space of
time in which to unfold and expand.[39] All art, therefore, is
temporal, and the old division between the temporal and spatial
arts is swept away as the sorry product of an aesthetics of the
art object. Yet what is most interesting here is not the temporality
of all art but the fashion in which time is perceived. In aesthetic
experience, objective time is replaced by psychological time,
hence the apparent timelessness of art. There is an apparent
suspension of linear, chronological time. In its place a temporal
movement in depth appears, a searching, vertical time, whose
speed is not mechanically constant but is rather a function of

---

[38] "For art comes to you proposing frankly to give nothing but the highest
quality to your moments as they pass, and simply for those 'moments' sake."

[39] Cf. J. Dewey, *Art as Experience*, p. 220.

perceptual movement. Art pauses and dips, rushes forward in a cascade of sensation, moves gently onward with undulating movement, or is suspended in perceptual space for an eternal moment. The variety of the temporal surface of art is as wide as perception itself.

To say that aesthetic experience is immediate, then, does not mean that it is fleeting. It is to utter a denial, to assert that there is no intermediary in our encounter with art. As qualitative experience, art is felt with a compelling directness in which detachment, deliberation, and all other intermediate states have no place. Symbol and substitute, therefore, do not yet exist, nor does propositional truth.[40] There is forceful presentation rather than representation. Sensory qualities predominate in their immediacy and directness, and even when experience intensifies to the degree of rapture or awe, sensation is not transcended but lies at its very heart. The experience of art is neither religious nor mystical; it is eminently worldly.[41] Not only are sensory qualities present in the immediacy of aesthetic experience; relations are often there as well. However they are felt rather than cognized in the context of qualitative immediacy which distinguishes the experience of art.[42] The qualitative nature of aesthetic experience, its sensuousness, and its immediacy thus complement one another.[43]

---

[40] Cf. John Hospers, *Meaning and Truth in the Arts* (Chapel Hill, University of North Carolina Press, 1946), pp. 175, 195; J. Stolnitz, *Aesthetics and Philosophy of Art Criticism* (Boston, Houghton, Mifflin, 1959), p. 319. The place of symbol, substitute, and truth in art are discussed later in this chapter.

[41] Cf. Suzanne Langer's discussion of transcendence in "Abstraction in Art," *Journal of Aesthetics and Art Criticism*, XXII, 4 (Summer 1964), pp. 390-1. Cf. also D. W. Gotshalk, *Art and the Social Order* (New York, Dover, 1962), p. 185.

[42] Cf. Dewey, *Art as Experience*, pp. 119 ff.

[43] Cf. Dewey, *Art as Experience*, p. 293. The immediacy of aesthetic experience combined with an empathic physical involvement has been associated with architecture. Geoffrey Scott has argued that ". . . art addresses us through immediate impressions rather than through the process of reflection, and this universal metaphor of the body . . . is its largest opportunity." *The Architecture of Humanism*, in M. Weitz, ed., *Problems in Aesthetics* (New York, Macmillan, 1959), p. 471. See also p. 469.

Intuitive

The immediacy of aesthetic experience not only denies that anything intrudes into the directness of our encounter with art; it also affirms the forceful presence of our experience. In its positive sense this is the intuitive quality of art.

Artists, anarchists that they are, seldom agree on their explanations of what art is about. It is all the more remarkable, then, to discover a striking convergence of opinion among creative artists on the intuitive force of art. At times aesthetic intuition is identified with vision, with insight, with a direct perception of what the world is, or if the artist is metaphysically inclined, with a direct perception of the nature of reality.

Like all the traits of aesthetic experience, intuition is unequally present in our experience of particular art forms and objects. Still, it appears in many different arts, each of which provides its own characteristic perception. Literature works over the situations of human life—man's relationships, passions, predicaments, the gamut of human involvements from birth to the ends of imagination. It leads us to an empathic awareness of these involvements. In writing about theater, one contemporary playwright sees theater providing us with "the immediate, personal, apprehension of truth—of the 'feel' of truth—about a thing, or a person, or a situation."[44] Art is not *like* experience, it is not a reflection or an imitation of real life, but it is *that very experience* in its most direct, forceful presence. Art, thus, is not a pallid reflection of life and of the world but the real thing in its purest and clearest form. When theater is at its best, we experience "the *feel* of what is true." We discover part of the actual experience of being a Jew, a Catholic, a Negro, a Communist, a homosexual, an alcoholic. We realize the power of the great human doubts, passions, crises, and relationships which we all undergo and thus all share. We are more real because other people are more real. We discover an ability, as Blake recognized,

> "To see the world in a grain of sand
> And heaven in a wild flower."

---

[44] Ossie Davis, "New Theater: Plays of Insight are Needed to Make Stage Vital in Our Lives," *The New York Times*, August 23, 1964, II, 1:1.

One of the elusive puzzles about artistic creation has been the place of inspiration in the process. Whatever the mechanism of the psychology of creation, descriptions of inspiration reveal the kind of direct insight, the immediate apprehension that is the hallmark of intuition. The intuitive is particularly pronounced in music, where there is nothing external to hang on to. The composer works largely by feel, by a sense of what is right. The innumerable decisions that he must make that are not determined by the refractoriness of his material, the limitations of his craft, or the conventions of his age, are guided by the sensitivity of his talent to the qualitative needs of the music.

We share this creative use of intuition in our appreciative engagement with art, adding to the essential unity of creator and perceiver. *Haiku* is an instance in which this identity is at its closest. Basho instructs the poet to catch the moment of inspiration and immediately put the experience into words.[45] Yet the poetics and the aesthetics of *haiku* merge, for its brief length and carefully specified form—three lines comprising seventeen syllables—encourage us to encompass it easily at once. This recalls Joyce's epiphanies. D. H. Lawrence applies a canon of intuition to the novel and to painting as well. "The knowing eye watches sharp as a needle; but the picture comes clean out of instinct, intuition and sheer physical action. Once the instinct and intuition gets into the brush tip, the picture *happens*, if it is to be a picture at all."[46] This is like what some painters call the "crying point," that point in a picture which sets the whole thing into effective action.

Aesthetic intuition may be thought of as the heart of aesthetic experience, yet it is often misunderstood or obscured. It is frequently confounded with experience that is mystical and with experience that is cognitive, although it differs radically from both these modes of experience. Mystical experience leaves the acute sensory awareness of art far behind on its transcendent journey to a plane of exalted illumination. In contrast, aesthetic awareness is open to and fully immersed in the movement of

---

[45] Makoto, Ueda, "Basho and the Poetics of *Haiku*," *J. of Aesthetics and Art Criticism*, XXI, 4 (Summer, 1963), pp. 424, 427.

[46] "Making Pictures," from *Assorted Articles*. Reprinted in B. Ghiselin, ed., *The Creative Process* (New York, New American Library, 1955), p. 69.

perceptual quality. It grasps directly the qualities of experience, never losing its intimate connection with the realm of sensation. Aesthetic intuition also differs sharply from intellectual intuition. Without resolving the question of whether it is ever possible to acquire dependable knowledge by means of intuitive procedures, such claims are often made for the immediacy of insight. Yet as we shall suggest next, aesthetic experience, for all its significance and profundity, never substantiates propositions for which we can claim literal truth. Moreover, the powerful sensory presence of aesthetic intuition is alien to the direct apprehension of propositional truth that is the distinctive mark of intellectual intuition.

Aesthetic intuition resembles what Whitehead has called *prehension*, "the process of appropriating into a unity of existence the many data presented as relevant by the physical processes of nature, resulting in the absolute, individual self-enjoyment that life implies."[47] The process by which we attain a unity of existence, however, is not an act of intellectual synthesis, just as the experience of art is not an analytic one. It is, to put it literally, preanalytic and presynthetic. While the activities of analysis and synthesis are largely reflective in character, aesthetic awareness takes place on a prereflective level, contextual rather than fragmented, and therefore undifferentiated by any conceptual distinctions. In its original sense, prehension is the seizing or grasping of something, and it is exactly this that happens in art. For aesthetic intuition is not only a psychological act; it involves what we might describe as a perceptual-motor intuition, an organic intuition. As we participate fully in the aesthetic relation, so we are not confined to cerebral activity. Rather we join in a full engagement that is free, direct, and spontaneous. It is this that receives special stress in the action painting of abstract expressionists like Pollack and de Kooning and in the introduction of chance elements into many of the contemporary arts. And it is this, too, that has been recognized by theories that stress the resemblance of art to play, and by arts that make literal use of features of play, like farce, Happenings, and some modern dance. Such a total engagement in

---

[47] *Modes of Thought* (1938) (New York, Free Press, 1966), pp. 150-151.

experience of all the dimensions of the human organism—the imaginative, rational, sensuous, impulsive—was perhaps what Schiller was identifying in his observation that "Man only plays when in the full meaning of the word he is a man, and he is only completely a man when he plays."

Noncognitive

Art, Cassirer has written, "is an interpretation of reality—not by concepts but by intuitions; not through the medium of thought but through that of sensuous forms."[48] It is with matters of knowledge that many of the most deeply rooted confusions in aesthetics lie. The claim that great art embodies profound meaning, that there is more "truth" in a fragile lyric than in a library of learned tomes, has been voiced so often that it has not only become a literary cliché but has been taken over by many writers on art as an unquestioned axiom of aesthetics, a brace against which aesthetic theory must be bent and fastened into conformity. Many recent as well as older writers have argued persistently and effectively for the presence of cognitive attributes in art such as knowledge, truth, and meaning. Some, like Plato and Tolstoy, have even assigned art a didactic function, especially for the transmission of moral knowledge. To deny categorically, then, that art has a cognitive dimension might be regarded as an aesthetic heresy. Although this is not the place to present the full case against the cognitivist position, the tendency to seek and to presume to find such things as truth in art is so widespread and is at the root of so many of the surrogate theories we have already discussed that it is necessary to offer some reasons for rejecting it.

The Aesthetic and Cognitive Modes of Experience

The force of aesthetic intuition, which brings us into direct confrontation with experience at its most immediate, tends to lead us too far. There is a fullness to our encounter with a wide range of experience in the arts, from the complexes of perceptual qualities that have no apparent referent, as in absolute music

---

[48] Ernst Cassirer, *Essay on Man* (Garden City, New York, Doubleday, 1956), p. 188.

and wholly abstract painting, to the particularity of human situations evoked by poetry, the novel, and drama which, when they succeed, possess a convincing ring of authenticity and a sharing of experience. These carry so profound a significance and so important an achievement, that to describe them we turn naturally to that mode of experience which traditionally has claimed the highest stature—cognitive experience.

It is unfortunate for the development of a genuine theory of art that an intellectual model has been taken as the standard for experience since the classical age of Greek philosophy. From Plato on through the eighteenth century and into the present, all experience has been forced into a cognitive mold. Whatever did not meet the criteria of knowledge was disparged as illusory, lowly, or otherwise inappropriate to the rational activity that is man's proper function. Aristotle, to take an influential example, began his *Metaphysics* with the famous statement, "All men by nature desire to know." Then he proceeded to account for the delight we take in our senses for their own sake by explaining that the senses, especially sight, are avenues to knowledge.

Yet human history since the fourth century B.C. has shown little to bear out this affirmation of man's essential rationality. The discovery of a pervasive and often hidden irrationality in the psychology of individuals and groups has caused us to perform a radical reassessment of ourselves. Yet to debate human rationality or irrationality assumes that questions of knowledge are primary, and this is precisely the point at issue. From what we have learned about human beings through the behavioral sciences, there is little cause to assign rationality a predominant place. It is never given but is, at most, an achievement, always limited and seldom frequent. It would be more accurate to say that all men appear to be born with the desire for experience. To state this does not prejudice the question of the nature of that experience; what it does do is oblige us to accept the primacy and authority that experience carries.

When we search for an answer to this question, however, we are led to recognize that experience, whatever the forms into which it may develop, is initially direct and uncategorized. When it is aesthetic, intuition takes one back before knowledge, before recognition. It makes one aware of the immediacy of experience and of the directness of one's response to it. That is why there is such a strong sensory factor in the experience of art. But when experience is given a cognitive turn, we move beyond the indiscriminate fullness of immediate experience to the selection of those data that will serve as evidence for sound and rational judgment, and on this evidence we construct arguments and perform inferences. Consequently, cognition leaves behind the living directness of sensory perception by using it as a means to conceptual conclusions and effective applications. Wordsworth realized this when he commented that we murder in order to dissect. To force aesthetic experience into a cognitive mold results in mistreating a kind of direct qualitative experience that is characteristically nondiscursive and hence nonrational. Art is the height of consciousness; cognition the height of self-consciousness.[49]

---

[49] The contention that aesthetic experience is noncognitive is not a new one. Kant, despite his antipathy to Hume's philosophy, agreed with him on this. Hume took beauty to be felt rather than perceived, so that any reasoning transforms it into something new and different. And while Kant was willing to speak of a judgment of taste, he argued that it was not a cognitive judgment, since it rested on subjective grounds. He claimed, in fact, that the beautiful is what pleases without concept. It is perhaps surprising, too, to discover how frequently the distinction between the immediacy of direct experience and the mediating cognitive operations performed on it has been made by philosophers. Among the pragmatists it occupies an important place. C. S. Peirce, for example, drew an important difference between objects of which we are immediately conscious and those of which we are mediately conscious. Among the first he included sensations, and among the second, thought ("How to Make Our Ideas Clear," in J. Buchler, ed. *Philosophical Writings of Peirce*, New York, Dover, 1955, p. 28). One of Dewey's most basic distinctions, occurring throughout his writings, especially those on logic, metaphysics, and aesthetics, is between the preanalytic phase and the reflective phase of experience. Dewey held that all direct experience is of a qualitative sort and possesses intrinsic value. When we reflect, however, we go beyond such immediate qualities, for we are interested in commensurable objects and in the relations that can be drawn among them. It is to the reflective process that logic and science devote themselves (Cf., for example, *Art as Experience*, pp. 145, 293). Croce, too, while using the cognitive category of knowledge, contrasted intuitive with logical knowledge. The intuitive is concerned with images of individual things, while in the logical, the intellect deals with universal concepts and relations between things (*Aesthetic*, New York, Macmillan, rev. ed, 1922, pp. 1, 15). Merleau-Ponty's distinction between the nonthetic and thetic experience of a situation resembles these, for he is discriminating prerational awareness from the intellectual determination of

This is not anti-intellectualism in aesthetics. It is rather a protest against the indiscriminate reduction of the manifold variety of experience to one of its particular modes, even though a mode of undeniable importance. By excluding the cognitive from aesthetic experience, however, we have focused on an important difference between the two. The process of reflection, of the manipulation of intellectual and physical tools directed toward the end of achieving warranted assertions, is one which is hardly direct. Cognition leads to the formulation of knowledge in propositions that are supported by adequate relevant evidence. It is an activity, therefore, whose value lies in the culmination of inference in sound conclusions. While aesthetic experience is direct and immediate, intellectual experience is mediated. It is, in a manner of speaking, the experience of experience (the secondary or derivative experience of primary experience). It requires an element of disengagement, of disinterestedness and impartiality. That is why features such as distance and contemplation are not characteristics of the aesthetic attitude but rather of the cognitive. Indeed, the codification of cognitive experience in factual statements is not the end of the process but an intermediate stage in the endless (nonterminating, in C. I. Lewis' term) task of testing and refining these conclusions in use.

---

structure and meanings of a situation. (*Phenomenology of Perception.* New York, Humanities Press, 1962, pp. 60 ff). An interesting version of the same type of distinction appears in Virgil Aldrich's *Philosophy of Art* (Englewood Cliffs, New Jersey, Prentice-Hall, 1963, pp. 21-24). Aldrich identifies two mutually exclusive modes of perception of objects. There is the aesthetic mode which he calls "prehension," in which characteristics such as qualities of sounds and colors create the spatial properties of things. In contrast, the mode of "observation" apprehends objects in physical space by their quantitative material characteristics. We can observe similar uses of this type of distinction in Zen Buddhism's contrast between *Prajna*, which is pure act, pure experience, and *Vijnana*, which is reason or discursive understanding, as well as in Korzybski's differentiation of the unspeakable objective level of immediate and direct emotional and mental reactions and reflexes from the verbal level (Alfred Korzybski, *Science and Sanity*, 4th ed., 1958, pp. 34-35). Erwin Straus also develops a corresponding contrast between sensing, which is individual and personal, and knowing, which, like perception, is objective, universally valid, and repeatable. He uses this to propose some suggestive comparisons between the space of landscape and the space of geography, natural sounds and musical ones, and the family of nature with the family of man (*The Primary World of Senses*, London, 1963, pp. 316-331).

The cognitive process, then, forever mediates between the aspirations of men and their present conditions. And knowledge, as the product of this process, acquires value through its ability to assist men in satisfying their desires. Aesthetic experience, on the other hand, is noncognitive in the sense of being pre-cognitive. It antecedes the dualism between the conceptual and the affective. As Aquinas observed, "Clarity is for beauty what evidence is for truth." We neither pause to analyze nor labor to prove. Like knowledge, art begins with immediate experience; unlike knowledge, art never passes beyond it.

It is striking to discover how frequently creative artists have commented on the remoteness of intellectual activity to the aesthetic situation. Degas, for example, disliked talking about his art. "What use is my mind? Granted that it enables me to hail a bus and pay my fare. But once I am inside my studio, what use is my mind? I have my model, my pencil, my paper, my paints. My mind doesn't interest me."[50] Joyce Cary applies the same idea to literature with complete forthrightness. "We have to have conceptual knowledge to organize our societies, to save our own lives, to lay down general ends for conduct, to engage in any activity at all, but that knowledge, like the walls we put up to keep out the weather, shuts out the real world and the sky. It is a narrow little house which becomes a prison to those who can't get out of it. The artist, the writer, simply in order to give his realization, his truth, has to break these walls, the conceptual crust."[51] In Kafka's terse phrase, "Art reveals a reality which surpasses our conceptual ability." And Whitman, on hearing the learn'd astronomer, rose and left and

---

[50] Quoted in Daniel Halévy, *My Friend Degas* (Middletown, Conn., Wesleyan University Press, 1964). Chagall's comment on his paintings reveals a similar attitude: "I don't understand them at all. They are not literature. They are merely pictorial arrangements of images that obsess me." Jean Cassou, *Chagall* (New York, Prager, 1965), p. 26.

[51] *Art and Reality* (Cambridge, 1958), p. 165. Plato gave classic expression to this in the *Ion* (534, 536), although his view was affected by the prominent position he gave to knowledge: "For the poet is an airy thing, a winged and a holy thing; and he cannot make poetry until he becomes inspired and goes out of his senses and no mind is left in him; so long as he keeps possession of this, no man is able to make poetry and chant oracles. Not by art [i.e. practical knowledge], then, they make their poetry with all those fine things about all sorts of matters . . . not by art, but by divine dispensation. . . ."

"Looked up in perfect silence at the stars." One discovers the identical attitude in still other arts. John Martin writes of Mary Wigman's magnificent aliveness and eloquence of body, of "her profundity of emotional penetration, and her ability to communicate her perceptions in the unintellectualized realm of experience," which combine to "make her dancing a thing of constant evocation. . . ."[52] Similarly, Balanchine insists on restricting dance to its own terms and opposes intellectualizing and interpreting it. And for music, Stravinsky's remark is succinct and wholly sufficient: "The one true comment on a piece of music is another piece of music."[53]

The Aesthetic Error

All this is not meant to disparage knowledge but rather to see its place in the broad spectrum of human activity in proper perspective. When we assert that art has meaning and truth, we doubtless intend to express something of genuine significance. Yet any literal claim to cognitive status results in rejecting the purely aesthetic nature of the artistic event and replacing it with a surrogate. To confound the reflective, analytic attitude with the aesthetic is to commit what we might call "the aesthetic error," and it is this confusion which is responsible in part for the low regard in which aesthetics is often held. This is what lies behind Valéry's criticism of the attempt to generalize about art and construct systems of aesthetics. He is indeed right to say that "the effect of the Beautiful upon a man to make him *mute!*"[54] Yet he has failed to note the crucial difference between the quite separate activities of apprehending, appreciating, and understanding art.

To *apprehend* art is to engage in a perceptual act, the act of perceiving an art object. It is the basic organic activity of experiencing, and is the prerequisite for every specific mode of engagement. To *appreciate* art is to engage in one particular

---

[52] *An Introduction to the Dance* (New York, Norton, 1939), p. 236.

[53] From an interview in the *New York Review of Books*, May 12, 1966, p. 12. Louis Armstrong agrees. On being asked to define New Orleans jazz, he replied, "Man, when you got to ask what it is, you'll never get to know."

[54] Paul Valéry, *Aesthetics, in Collected Works,* Vol. 13 (New York, Bollingen, 1964), p. ix.

way of apprehending it, a specifically aesthetic way. Appreciating art means participating in an aesthetic field and therefore experiencing an object aesthetically. It is the appreciation or the aesthetic experience of art that is the source of the data with which aesthetic theory deals. To *understand* art is to theorize about it, and it is this that is the proper business of aesthetics. It is a reflective, cognitive activity of identifying and analyzing the data, formulating appropriately relevant abstractions, and developing explanatory hypotheses about the nature and meanings of art.

Although aesthetic theory comes out of the appreciative experience of art, it also feeds back into it, helping us to participate with art in a clearer, more direct way, less distracted by considerations that are inappropriate. It also helps us identify the data in the creation, performance, and criticism of art that are relevant for appreciation. In addition, many related disciplines offer important assistance to aesthetic theory, fields such as the psychology of art, the history of the arts, and the sociology of art.

These distinctions between apprehending, appreciating, and understanding art are basic ones, yet they are often overlooked, as in the case of those who do not like modern art "because it doesn't make any sense," or ridicule contemporary music because they "don't understand it." Such bewilderment or lack of comprehension may be genuine and understandable, but it is a quite different matter from the absence of appreciation. Delacroix once observed that "before learning what the picture represents you are seized by its magical accord." Appreciation generally precedes cognitive understanding, not the converse. In fact it even precedes the act of recognition. It is often true that commentators and critics may provide us with sufficient knowledge of what a particular artist is attempting, so as to help us leap over the conceptual obstacles to our appreciation. Yet the ideas by which he leads us to sympathetic appreciation themselves derive their insight and success through the perceptions he has gained from his own aesthetic enjoyment. Theory and explanation can never create appreciation; they can at most make it possible. And their validity is a direct consequence of the authenticity of their source. It is a typically aesthetic error to confuse the reflective, analytic attitude of the cognitive approach to art with the appreciative one of the experience of art.

All this suggests the way in which the critic can make a genuine contribution to the aesthetic event. By informed and discerning judgment, the good critic must not only accept his subordinate role in the world of art but must recognize the qualitative difference between the cognitive activity of criticism and the creative immediacy of aesthetic experience. He, so to speak, *represents* in conceptual terms what the artist originally *presents* in perceptual ones. This distinction might be said to conform to the difference between the preanalytic phase and the reflective phase of aesthetic experience.[55] Geoffrey Scott put this point well when he wrote,

> The true task of criticism is to understand such aesthetic pleasures as have in fact been felt, and then to draw whatever laws and conclusions it may from that understanding. But no amount of reasoning will create, or can annul, an aesthetic experience; for the aim of the arts has not been logic, but delight.[56]

The function of criticism in the arts is, however, a subject that warrants fuller discussion in its own right, and I shall turn to this in the next chapter.

Knowledge in Art

As a cognitive discipline in its own right, aesthetic theory derives from the practice of art and serves its need for reflective understanding. Yet when we separate the function of aesthetics from the experience of art, we are compelled to reject interpretations of art as an expressive, communicative, linguistic, symbolic, or otherwise cognitive activity. Although this rejection carries with it important consequences, it does not mean, however, that the aesthetic and the intellectual are antithetical activities, nor does it imply that they are irreconcilable.

While it is misleading to conceive of art as a form or source of knowledge, knowledge of different sorts has considerable relevance to the several phases of aesthetic experience. This,

[55] John Dewey, *Art as Experience* (New York, Capricorn Books) pp. 145, 293.

[56] *The Architecture of Humanism,* in M. Weitz, ed., *Problems in Aesthetics* (New York, Macmillan, 1959), p. 467.

however, is not knowledge that is provided by art but rather knowledge that is required and used in artistic activities. There is craftsmanship, which includes knowledge of the materials and techniques that are used in handling an artistic medium, as well as facility with them. The creative artist acquires a vast store of such knowledge, some of it during his apprenticeship, much of it from the sheer experience of working in his art, and he evolves his own style partly from such knowledge. A composer, to take one example, may learn or develop his own techniques for thematic transformation, from diminution to augmentation, inversion and cancrizans, and he may apply them to fugal forms, using serial techniques or in some other way. So, too, does he develop knowledge of musical forms, harmony, orchestration and instrumental writing, and to this he may add the understanding of recording technology and electronic music synthesizers. Some composers constantly grow in their technical knowledge, while others remain content to work within certain limits.

The element of skill undoubtedly plays a significant part in the achievement of any artist. Limits in craftsmanship often turn into limitations in achievement, as with Schubert and Schumann. Both were superb miniaturists, excelling in lieder and short piano pieces, but were hampered when they turned to more extended musical forms. Often they were unable to elaborate upon their melodic inventiveness, and resorted to simple repetition in different keys instead of working out and developing their materials. One striking example of this is the finale of Schubert's *Piano Trio in Eb*, op. 100, in which extended melodic material is arranged in sonata-allegro form. The result is that the movement goes on for thirty pages in which lovely themes are repeated so frequently that they become first tiresome and then ludicrous.

Many of the same requisites for knowledge apply to musical performers, who need to know a large variety of things, from fingering patterns to the rendering of ornaments and the styles of interpretation that are customary and appropriate to different periods. These kinds of knowledge may be transferred to the listener as well. To the extent that he is versed in music theory, composition, and performance, he is able to participate creatively in the ongoing musical process. Through a kind of detailed sensitivity to what is happening, his perceptiveness increases and his response is enhanced. An educated listener hears more in a purely quantitative sense, by being able to perceive not just sounds but their treatment, patterns, distribution, and relationships as well. Moreover, what we have been saying about musical knowledge is but a single instance that could be applied as readily, *mutatis mutandis,* to any other art.

Furthermore, there are cases in which prior knowledge is actually necessary for us to apprehend some art objects aesthetically. Literature requires knowledge of a language and sensitivity to subtle differences of inflection and vocabulary. One needs no knowledge of Russian to listen appreciatively to Prokofieff's *Fifth Symphony,* but the same could hardly be said of reading *Anna Karénina* in the original. The difficulties of translating a masterful work of literature are a clear confirmation of this. Painting that is representational may require familiarity with the subject matter of the work and skill in responding to objects and symbols, together with an awareness of conventions representing such perceptual features as depth. Such knowledge contributes to the aesthetic act and response only when it is relevant to the experience and enhances it, without deflecting attention to the cognitive rather than the appreciative. To do otherwise is, so to speak, to unload one's intellectual baggage onto the dance stage.[57]

Finally, however, while cognitive awareness may be a condition for aesthetic experience under some circumstances, the appreciative engagement often occurs more directly without the aid of knowledge and training. This is usually when the sensory dimensions of art are emphasized most strongly. It may occur when one first attends a ballet performance and is entranced by the visual spectacle of bodily motion and the sensuality

---

[57] Stolnitz makes the point neatly: "'Knowledge about' is relevant under three conditions: when it does not weaken or destroy aesthetic attention to the object, when it pertains to the meaning and expressiveness of the object, and when it enhances the quality and significance of one's immediate aesthetic response to the object. . . . This is the great danger in all 'Knowledge about' art—that it will remain external to the work, that it will, indeed, divert attention away from the work. This is, precisely, aesthetic irrelevance." *Aesthetics and Philosophy of Art Criticism* (Boston, 1958), pp. 58-59.

that can never be completely divorced from the human form. It may happen when one feels the texture of a fabric, or perhaps half mystically abandons himself to the caress of sunlight or to the panoramic spectacle from a mountain without making any effort at recognition or identification.[58] Some of the contemporary arts exercise their appeal in this way. By means of a powerful sensory impact, they impose a demand for our exclusive attention, and enclose us in a sensory environment that pushes thought aside in favor of a direct apprehension of quality. An environment such as Lucas Samaras' "Mirrored Room" in the Albright-Knox Art Gallery in Buffalo fascinates us with an endless series of reflections radiating out from ourselves in all directions, so that we lose sight of our recognizable identity and dissolve into nothing but a central source of multidimensional visual patterns. A rather different case occurs through the use of electronic instruments and amplification by various rock music groups. The tendency to turn the volume to a deafening level results in our being encased in an environment of sound to the exclusion of all reflective distance.[59]

The Symbol in Art

The relation of knowledge to the appreciation of art objects is, as we see, a complex one, and many more issues can be raised here than resolved. We have seen how the artist requires knowledge in his craft and how prior knowledge is sometimes necessary for full appreciation. Thus the activities that generate aesthetic experience make use of knowledge of many sorts, even though the experience itself does not provide any. There is one problem, however, which it would be helpful to explore more closely since it bears in many ways upon the ideas I am developing, and that is the aesthetic relevance of symbols. This in itself is a question too large to examine here with the fullness it deserves. Yet the view that art has cognitive content is often seen to rest on the fact that symbols can be discovered in art

---

[58] Cf. D. H. Parker, *The Principles of Aesthetics* (New York, Appleton-Century-Crofts, 2nd ed., 1946), pp. 46-48.

[59] The contemporary arts are taken as a case study in the application of the aesthetic theory developed here in A. Berleant, "Aesthetics and the Contemporary Arts," *J. of Aesthetics and Art Criticism*, forthcoming.

objects, particularly in pictorial and literary ones. It would seem that the presence of symbols in art and the claim that appreciation requires us to be aware of them are a clear refutation of the noncognitive character of art.

The search for symbols is itself, however, an expression of the intellectual fascination that the arts exert on us. We are intrigued by questions that probe into the "meaning" of literary and pictorial characters and events. The richness of classical mythology has supplied two millenia with powerful dramatic figures—Prometheus, Antigone, Oedipus, and a host of others. As they are types rather than individuals, we find ourselves asking about the source of their literary force. What, we wonder, is the larger meaning of the Oedipus tragedy? Does Oedipus represent man's defiance of fate? Prometheus man's challenge to the hegemony of the gods? Antigone man's disobedience of the state in deference to a higher law? Dissatisfied with accepting these as literal tales, we find ourselves searching for their greater significance. Examples are as varied as literature, and the question persists. Sometimes it is made explicit, as when Tennyson asks of the flower in the crannied wall,

> Little flower—but if I could understand
> What you are, root and all, and all in all,
> I should know what God and Man is.

At other times the symbolism is veiled, as in the case of Kafka's protagonist "K," in *The Trial* and *The Castle*. Much of the literature that is associated with the existentialist movement possesses strong overtones of more general significance. *Nausea* is about more than Roquentin, Mersault is not alone *The Stranger*, and Greek mythological symbols are regenerated in *The Myth of Sisyphus* and *The Flies*. Many situations, too, possess an import that breaches their literal limits, as in Kafka's *Metamorphosis* and *In the Penal Colony*, and in Sartre's *No Exit*. In painting, the search for meaning has become so developed that it has evolved into the separate discipline of iconography. Art historians and critics find it essential to unravel the significance of the component images in paintings in order to reveal their total import. The meaning of some images is common cultural knowledge in the West, as of the cross, the figure of

Christ, Moses and the Tablets of the Law, and the Last Supper. Others require special knowledge for us to realize their allegorical significance, as when in religious art the lambs are Christians, the fish or the vine Christ, peacocks immortality, and a lily the virginity of Mary. Still others require scholarship of enormous breadth, as we can see in Erwin Panofsky's explication of Dürer's "Melencolia I." With such impressive evidence for the importance and pervasiveness of symbols in the arts, how is it possible to take issue with their aesthetic status?

This question, however, is not rhetorical. In denying that symbols are cognitive objects in art, I am not denying any of the facts that appear so convincing. The power of mythical figures, the impact of certain situations and objects, are facts of aesthetic experience and they demand an explanation. Yet claiming that these are symbols does not offer a fact but rather an explanation. Moreover it is an explanation that is the consequence of accounting for art by means of a surrogate theory, one that confounds aesthetic experience with the reflective activity of cognition. Thus the problem is confused rather than clarified. Yet how, then, can symbols be accounted for?

"Symbol," to begin, is a cognitive concept. It is an invaluable tool in the construction and transmission of meaning, encompassing language, logic, mathematics, certain gestures used in communication, and much more. Symbols function as mechanisms for ordering the multifarious data of experience and manipulating it indirectly. Quite literally, a symbol "throws together" an object, a situation, an event, or even an idea with a sign denoting it. By using the sign in place of the object it denotes, we acquire a range of discourse that goes far beyond that of Swift's men of Laputa, who sought to avoid the pitfalls of language by dispensing with it entirely and conversing exclusively by means of objects they carried in sacks on their backs. Thus with a word we can, in thought, erect skyscrapers, dam rivers, destroy civilizations, arrange and rearrange all the things in our worlds and our lives. Symbols, then, are enormously powerful means for going beyond whatever we have at hand, the better to control them.

Yet art, as we have seen, enables us to achieve a directness and immediacy of experience which symbols, by their very nature, seek to transcend. To attempt to reconcile the immediacy of experience in art with the mediacy of symbolic uses is to embroil oneself in an irresolvable contradiction. Matthew Arnold struggled with this when he described words as "symbols equivalent with the thing symbolized," and it is the same predicament that Suzanne Langer finds herself in with her notion of presentational symbol.[60] At times, we defer to the cognitive commitments of aesthetics by speaking of artistic symbols as expressive symbols. Yet these concepts are all theoretical constructions which obscure the often sensitive observations of those who make use of them. We would do far better to dispense with cognitive concepts like "symbol" and "meaning" entirely rather than twist them into unrecognizable shapes so that they will conform to the facts of aesthetic experience. Literally, they are intermediaries; figuratively, they introduce confusion and disorder. Thus iconographic symbols, presentational symbols, and expressive symbols join ideographic symbols; as symbols they obtrude on the direct experience of art. Through their offices the intellectual fascination with the arts is transformed into the intellectual bias of aesthetics. Paul Klee was right in observing that "Art does not render the visible; rather it *makes visible.*" Artistic symbols do not *do;* they *are.*

Yet if we admit all this, how can we account for the larger

---

[60] Despite her remarkable knowledge and sensitivity to philosophical issues in art, Langer is saddled with the notion of symbol, which she must somehow force into conformity with the presentational immediacy of aesthetic experience. Symbol is conjoined in her view with the primacy of form, and together they make odd bedfellows with the presentational directness and sensuousness of appearance. In her efforts to extend logic to encompass the artistic symbol, Langer offers a striking example of a consistently developed surrogate theory of art. And the surrogate wins out over the art when she asserts that "what art expresses is *not* actual feeling, but ideas of feeling; as language does not express actual things and events but ideas of them." Yet her struggles at reconciliation continue uneasily when she insists later in the same paragraph that "a purely and wholly articulated symbol *presents* its import directly to any beholder who is sensitive at all to articulated forms in the given medium." (*Feeling and Form* [New York, Scribner's, 1953], p. 59.) Cf. the insightful criticism of Langer's semantic theory of art by Ernest Nagel (*Logic Without Metaphysics* [Glencoe, Ill., Free Press, 1956], pp. 353-360) and Richard Rudner's more general critique of semiotic theories (*Aesthetic Inquiry,* ed. M. C. Beardsley and H. M. Schueller, Belmont, Cal., Dickenson, 1967, pp. 93-102).

significance of the images and objects that art objects contain? Putting aside the intellectual quests of the scholar and the critic and returning to the actual experience of art, an answer begins to emerge. For what is important here is how what we call on reflection symbols actually *function* in aesthetic experience. Their forcefulness does not lie in the identifications we can consciously make but rather in the quality of experience to which they contribute. *The symbol functions aesthetically,* not as an intellectual object which facilitates the analysis of meaning, *but as a vehicle for the direct perception of an identity between it and the object symbolized.* It is a metaphor in scholar's robes. When we apprehend this identity with intuitive immediacy, the symbol has been employed successfully. When it must be made explicit, it fails in its artistic function. Joyce Cary, still encumbered by surrogate terms, has spoken of "the charged symbol, at once concept and experience."[61]

If the artistic symbol were to function as a literal symbol, it would incur the disabilities that befall the imitation theory of art. Its significance in an art object would be derivative, depending upon its referent rather than upon its intrinsic import, just as an imitative work parasitically must draw its sustenance from the object it represents. In its artistic use, however, the symbol becomes more like a substitute, a replacement for its referent. As such it is self-sufficient and thus actually no longer a symbol.[62] Rather it is like a totem with which one has a subservient kinship relationship and identifies himself. This is far different from the offices of a symbol by which an object can be controlled. Relevance a symbol has, yet it is experiential relevance rather than referential relevance. Nor does the symbol actually become a substitute for its referent; at most it merges with it, being at

---

[61] *Art and Reality*, p. 174.

[62] Cf. E. H. Gombrich's treatment of this point in "Meditations on a Hobby Horse or the Roots of Artistic Form," in *Aspects of Form*, ed. by L. L. Whyte (London, Lund Humphries, 1951). Cf. also Cassirer, who maintains that "art is, indeed, symbolism, but the symbolism of art must be understood in an immanent, not in a transcendent sense." (*Essay on Man*, p. 201.) Douglas Morgan has also given an excellent argument for the significance of art independent of cognitive, scientific, or informational truth. Knowing occurs by sympathetic union with what is known. Cf. "Must Art Tell the Truth?," *Journal of Aesthetics and Art Criticism*, XXVI, 1 (1967), pp. 17-27.

once itself, the object, and the essence of the object, in an experience that has translucent depths.

Aesthetic perception, when it is successfully connected with ideas, brings us back to the noncognitive perceptual root of our concepts and beliefs. It evokes the sensory significance of ideas. Here abstract concepts recede into the background and pre-reflective sensory apprehension predominates.[63] This process has certain affinities with Jung's description of what he terms the visionary mode of artistic creation, "a primordial experience which surpasses man's understanding . . ." and makes contact with the common but hidden source of conscious knowledge.[64] Ideas can not really be separated from the force of their presentation. In the lecture, in the essay, and especially in the literary arts there is a dramatic power that accompanies the development of an idea. Take these away and there is left nothing at all. So far as an idea is thought, it assumes sensuous garb; it lives in human experience and is fused with the vital force of biological consciousness. An exclusively neutral concept is the fiction of the rationalist and the logician.[65]

Thus what is regarded as a symbol in a painting or a novel is not literally symbolic. As symbol, an object, place, or event would have to stand for something other than itself. It would present a problem which had to be solved before the entire art object could be experienced and enjoyed fully. Yet this makes

---

[63] This corresponds to what H. H. Price calls "primary recognition," in contrast to "secondary recognition" which is the ordinary perception of familiar objects that goes beyond the directly perceived color or shape to deal with them in logical or epistemological terms. Cf. *Thinking and Experience* (London, Hutchinson's, 1953), pp. 44-51.

[64] Cf. *Modern Man in Search of a Soul* (1933) (New York, Harcourt-Brace), pp. 156-157. This, of course, does not entail accepting the notion of a collective unconscious. There is some resemblance, too, between my treatment of symbols and Jung's use of anagogic symbols which refer to the moral or allegorical tendencies of the unconscious.

[65] Stephen Spender makes a similar point: "If the line embodies the ideas which I have related . . . these ideas must be further made clear in other lines. That is the terrifying challenge of poetry. Can I think out the logic of images? How easy it is to explain here the poem that I would have liked to write! How difficult it would be to write it. For writing it would imply living my way through the imaged experience of all these ideas, which here are mere abstractions, and such an effort of imaginative experience requires a lifetime of patience and watching." "The Making of a Poem," *Partisan Review*, XIII (1946), p. 3.

the challenge of art into an intellectual pastime—a reverse crossword puzzle in which the answer is given and the explanation must be supplied. If we regard the experience of art as noncognitive, however, the putative symbol must be treated differently. This may seem a difficult thing to do, but it is so only if we allow ourselves to be encumbered with a cognitive object which has somehow to be shown to be noncognitive. When we turn to the symbol as it functions in the aesthetic field, the problem becomes much less obstinate. What once was a symbol becomes something taken as it is in itself. The fox in D. H. Lawrence's novel is not a symbol of the male but a cunning and vital creature; the dog and bat in Dürer's "Melencolia I" are not emblems of melancholy but, as Panofsky puts it, "living creatures, one squeaking with evident ill will, the other shrivelled up with general misery."

Yet surely such figures as these are not chosen arbitrarily. When recognizable, they must certainly have a special place in the total art object. By denying that they are cognitive objects or symbols, we are not therefore denying their importance. What then is the aesthetic function of objects that are commonly interpreted symbolically?

It is possible to identify at least three such functions, all of which may operate concurrently. First, the object may be the *central feature* that colors the entire situation. It may be the figures of the Virgin and Child in an adoration scene, the form of Christ in a Descent from the Cross, the subject in a portrait, the protagonist in a novel. Here the putative symbol exercises formal dominance over the entire artistic landscape, and the qualities that it evokes pervade the total field. If we described the object verbally, we would betray its aesthetic impact. To characterize van Eyck's *Annunciation* as representing hope and expectation or Leonardo's *Virgin and Child with St. Anne* as depicting maternal love and warmth is to misguide our perception into conventional abstractions instead of allowing us to participate in the wonder of experience that is qualitatively unique yet into which we can enter with human sympathy.

A second and more characteristic function of an object usually interpreted as a symbol is for it to serve as a *key element* in giving identity to a situation, summarizing it for recollection. Resembling the first symbolic function in exuding a unifying quality over the entire art object, this function differs in that the supposed symbol is no longer the central element but is instead an abbreviation for it. Acting as a metonym, it conjures up an aura of feeling and significance associated with it, as the "A" in Hawthorne's *Scarlet Letter* does to a puritanical society for which adultery is one of the most heinous of sins, or as the subtle layers of association do among which the blackbird flits in Wallace Steven's "Thirteen Ways of Looking at a Blackbird."[66] Whether an artificial object or a natural one, these are not cognitive symbols separate from their referents. Rather they are reified evocations united with the contexts in which they appear. Thus Maritain, invoking St. Thomas, describes poetic knowledge as making use of similitudes and symbols "in order to *seduce the reason*," since what they deal with cannot be conceptualized.[67] To seek logical explication is to overlook the functioning of such "symbols" in the sensuous context of aesthetic experience. When we extrapolate supposed symbols, we place them in the service of a cognitive end and thus distort them.

There is a third function of objects commonly described as symbols that is more diffuse than those we have just discussed, but which may well account for the greater part of the power such objects exert in the experience of art. It rests on *the basic union between the perceptual and feeling qualities of art objects and those same qualities as they combine outside art* to make up the full range of human perceptual experience. This identity

---

[66] This poem is a prime example of the way in which the commitment to a symbolic interpretation leads critics to search for intellectual consistency. Assuming that the blackbird is a symbol of something, they attempt to test a series of lyric images by the criterion for a logical proof. It seems never to occur to them that the directions explicit in the title might suffice. For a discussion of the difficulties in symbolically interpreting this poem, see Monroe Beardsley, *Aesthetics: Problems in the Philosophy of Criticism* (New York, Harcourt, Brace and World, 1958), pp. 401-403, 405-406, 407-408. Despite Beardsley's conclusion that there seems to be nothing that the blackbird can be taken to symbolize throughout the entire poem, he nonetheless maintains that there remains a *claim* to symbolic meaning upon which the poem constantly verges.

[67] "Concerning Poetic Knowledge," in Jacques and Raissa Maritain, *The Situation of Poetry* (New York, Philosophical Library, 1955).

precedes any distinctions that may be drawn later between the experiences of art and those of daily living or between the fine and the practical arts. Here lines, shapes, forms, colors, the inflections of the human voice, the contours of melodies, the pulse of rhythms, the choir of harmonious sound, all these material and formal aspects of artistic media possess a profound force to create reverberations in the great but hidden backlog of human experience.[68] Sartre once observed that the meaning in a painting is neither a sign nor a symbol nor even an image, and he extolled Guardi's pictorial evocations of Venice over Canaletto's perfect representations. While Canaletto's brush is subservient to the claims of appearances, Guardi, because of his sole concern with the plastic properties of light and color, succeeds in presenting Venice in his canvases "as it has been experienced by everyone and seen by no one."[69] This creativity in the perception and use of artistic materials explains why widely varying interpretations can be made of the same art object, why ambiguity of literal meaning and even blatant contradiction are tolerable. Aesthetic experience, because it is prelogical, concerns the human perceptual *experience* of meaning rather than its cognitive apprehension. Hence we will embrace in a novel what we would dismiss in a lecture.

Gestalt psychologists have shown how expressive qualities are intrinsic properties of all perception. These physiognomic properties, as they call them, unite the perception with the object into a dynamic expressive apprehension of things. Thus angular lines possess a sharpness and restiveness quite unlike the gentle softness inherent in undulating curves. The same presence of expressive features appears in our apprehension of different masses and spaces, which we recognize in the various feeling qualities that individual rooms and buildings possess.

While these expressive qualities are perceptually everywhere, art objects present more clearly and forcefully than anywhere else the human significance of perceptual qualities. It is for

---

[68] Camus has written that however exactly we translate or think we translate a symbol, only the artist himself can give it movement. "There is no word-for-word correspondence . . . a symbol always goes beyond him who would use it."

[69] *Essays in Aesthetics* (New York, Philosophical Library, 1963), p. 67.

this reason that we are inclined to attribute symbolic meaning to art. "In great works of art," Arnheim has written, "the deepest significance is transmitted to the eye with powerful directness by the perceptual characteristics of the compositional pattern," as in the scene depicting the creation of Adam on Michelangelo's Sistine ceiling. Passivity, movement, desire, life emerge from the pictorial surface through the skillful use of line, composition, and color, and the essential message of the story arises directly from the perceptual pattern of the painting. "The forces that characterize the meaning of the story become active in the observer, and produce the kind of stirring participation that distinguishes artistic experience from the detached acceptance of information."[70]

Yet there is more here than the immediate apprehension of a particular story. The great themes of art reflect the powerful moments of human life, those times when there is the least sham, hypocrisy, and evasion. Birth and the creation of life, the rich and complex network of relationships that entangle the human family, the tribulations of love, the ties between man and society, the direction and use of our lives, the final encounter with death—such subjects as these create reverberations in our private memories and cultural traditions, and their artistic presentations thus acquire concreteness in their statement and at the same time generality in their references. It is here that the individuality of particular experience merges with the universal depths of our common human natural being. From this comes the wonder of Dürer's "Hands in Prayer," whose lines, creases, and veins give them a unique identity, and yet whose expressive shape and common form bind them not only to all men's hands but to the human experience of reverence, peace, and awe as well. This is true not just of representational art but also of the magical drawing of Klee and the expressionist canvases of Kandinsky. For the world of fantasy, feeling, sense and imagination is as real phenomenally as the world of human action, and it too finds form in the particular constructions of creative men.

---

[70] Rudolf Arnheim, *Art and Visual Perception* (Berkeley and Los Angeles, University of California Press, 1954), Ch. X, esp. pp. 436-437.

This power of the arts lies beneath the surface of descriptive language and pet theories. It is a vital, precognitive force that emerges when we stand naked and honest, without our conventions or our other defenses to insulate us. This is the strength of art to purify, to reveal, to heal and rebuild human experience on a genuine foundation. Here we leave cognitive symbols far behind, and enter a region of direct experience, where all objects, all forms, all perceptual qualities are free to flow and intermingle with us. Here is the final relevance of art to life. Both merge on the level of authentic experience, and where there was once thought to be conflict there now emerges a fundamental harmony. Thus in the final analysis we can see a basic connection between the precognitive experience of art and the functional aspect of art. There is vital movement both in and between aesthetic perception and the full sphere of human activity, and each, when seen at its most inclusive, turns out to engage the other.[71]

Unique

To speak of art as unique is, on the surface, hardly to make a new observation or take issue with an old one. Uniqueness is perhaps one of the least controversial features of art, and most writers appear to agree on this if on nothing else. Still, like much accord, this is in part merely verbal, covering a measure of both confusion and disagreement.

First we must determine what it is that we are calling unique. Usually it is the art object that is meant. Great works of art, it is held, are singular creations, and part of their significance lies in the fact that each work has its own peculiar identity and occupies a special place in the corpus of art. Yet a statement such as this, tritely conventional as it may appear, not only masks confusion but fails to account for the facts. How great is our distress when we discover that a painting we had taken to be a Vermeer is really by van Meegeren, or that Kreisler's performances of Tartini and Corelli were really of his own

---

[71] A clear and useful discussion of the relation of truth and intellectual acts to aesthetic experience appears in Friedrich Kainz, *Aesthetics the Science,* trans. by Herbert M. Schueller (Detroit, Wayne State University Press, 1962), pp. 75-82, 132-135.

compositions! Do we admire the individuality of a painting or an artist, a sonata or a composer? It is similar with fraudulent copies of valuable originals. The case is further complicated by multicopy works, such as numbered lithographs or woodcuts taken from the same stone or block, or indistinguishable copies of the same statue, as of Michaelangelo's *David* or Rodin's *Balzac*. And when we come to consider works for which there is no original, as with art like posters and recordings that is produced in large quantities using industrial techniques of mass production instead of the handiwork of artist-craftsmen, with works such as marbles fashioned by expert stone cutters from clay models made by the sculptor, bronzes cast by craftsmen rather than the sculptor, metal sculptures fabricated according to plans or paper models made by artists such as David Smith and Picasso, or, to take a still different case, musical or dramatic works in which the performance rather than the score or script is the art object, we begin to realize the difficulties that develop from the attempt to apply the seemingly uncontroversial notion of uniqueness to art.

The problems that arise out of the innocent attempt to describe art as unique lead us to ask whether we may not be ascribing uniqueness to the wrong thing. We can take a long step toward resolving some of these difficulties if we were to speak of the uniqueness of aesthetic experience instead of the uniqueness of the art object. While the aesthetic field reveals a structural similarity in our experiences of art, the resemblance is formal only. In each of its occurrences aesthetic experience possesses a different and individual identity, for every experience in its pure, qualitative immediacy is unique and ineffable. Since its initial phase is phenomenal, even the existence of the world of objects is not presumed, a fact which led Dewey to call aesthetic perception "naturalistic" as opposed to "realistic."[72]

Because it occurs as singular occasions, aesthetic experience cannot be abstracted without being transformed into something entirely different. And without symbolization it cannot be communicated in any literal sense of the word. This is no

---

[72] *Art as Experience*, pp. 152-154. Cf. also pp. 191-192ff.

special feature of aesthetic experience though; it holds true for all perceptual experience, since it is initially direct and immediate. Some kinds of experiences, like cognitive, leave this behind, using it merely as a starting point. Aesthetic experience, along with mystical and religious experience, remains at this basic and direct level. Santayana took note of this ineffable uniqueness when he wrote that "Beauty as we feel it is something indescribable: what it is or what it means can never be said. . . . It is an experience: there is nothing more to say about it."[73] Under such conditions there is neither abstraction nor generality. "Language and science," Cassirer once wrote, "are abbreviations of reality; art is an intensification of reality. Language and science depend upon one and the same process of abstraction; art may be described as a continuous process of concretion."[74]

Here then is part of our answer. The uniqueness of art is the uniqueness of experience, not of object. If we acknowledge this, we can accept and explain those data that appeared so problematic at first. If we set aside aesthetically irrelevant interests, such as the concern of the collector for authenticity, of the historian for accuracy, of the art dealer for reliability, there is nothing troublesome about the uniqueness of art. The field in which each object of art is an element possesses its own experiential qualities, and aesthetically it is its own justification. This is equally the case with multicopy works and with works fabricated by others. This last is becoming more difficult to decide, since the cooperative production of art is increasingly important, as in architecture and film. And when we approach the performing arts where there is no perceptual original that is permanently extant, we can see the ease with which we can acknowledge their uniqueness. Here, Happenings, which are often created for but a single performance, simply carry out the promise implicit in musical and theatrical improvisation, and indeed in the performing arts *per se*.

Furthermore, uniqueness is often confounded with such different things as individuality, originality, and rarity. We speak of rarity when we are talking again about objects, not

---

[73] *The Sense of Beauty* (Scribner's, 1896), pp. 267, 268.

[74] *Essay on Man* (Garden City, Doubleday Anchor Books, 1956), p. 184.

experiences, and hence it has little place in an experiential aesthetics. Moreover, rarity is of perhaps greater importance in an economics of art than in a philosophy of art, for it is one of the primary sources of the commercial value of art objects. Even here, as Mumford has noted, rarity has largely historical importance and is becoming obsolescent in an industrial age when a large number of prints can be made of a motion picture film or pressings of a phonograph record.[75] Speaking in experiential terms, all art is equally rare, regardless of the number of identical objects which can function aesthetically.

Originality and individuality, too, mean something different in art from uniqueness. They involve interests which are historical and analytical rather than strictly aesthetic. We may have a legitimate concern with lines of influence among artists as individuals and in schools. The degree of innovation or derivativeness may tell us something about the artists themselves, but it is unimportant for aesthetic theory except insofar as it has an effect on our experience of art. Such an effect this surely has, but much has yet to be written on the historical dynamics of artistic originality and its influence on aesthetic perception.

Originality and individuality are capable of degrees. They have a good deal to do with the discovery of new perceptual regions and with the commentary of the artist as an explorer and critic of the quality of human life. Here his influence on aesthetic experience may be profound, and artistic originality is one of the sources of freshness and vitality in the arts. Individuality and originality in the arts also have much to do with some extra-aesthetic considerations. The value placed on individuality is bound up with romantic conceptions of the artist as cultural hero and with the psychology of artistic creation, and originality both affects and responds to styles in public taste. These, however, are questions for the historical sociology and the psychology of art, and are not the direct concern of its philosophy.

Intrinsic

Whereas the cognitive process is a means to the goal of knowledge which is itself primarily instrumental, the aesthetic

---

[75] *Technics and Civilization* (New York, Harcourt Brace, 1934), p. 353.

process is not. Aesthetic experience forces us to break out of the web of means in which our lives are entangled. For aesthetic perception is *intrinsic* perception, perception in itself and for its own sake, and the experience of art is sufficient in itself. When experience is direct and immediate, when it is thoroughly qualitative, it remains immersed in the perceptual sphere. It dwells on sense qualities and possesses a heightened sensibility, a clear sensitivity to the nuances in the wide range of organic and psychological activity and response by which an acute perceiver engages himself with art. Such intrinsic experience has a self-sufficiency; it is its own justification. Leading nowhere beyond itself, it never leaves itself behind. Aesthetic perception is essential perception, perception at its fullest and most complete.[76]

A great many notions prevalent in aesthetics reflect the influence of this feature of aesthetic experience, and it implies some interesting consequences. One way in which this intrinsic quality of art has been expressed is by describing great art as timeless, having eternal significance. This, however, confounds an honorific designation with a perceptual one. Any reference to the timelessness of aesthetic perception is, strictly speaking, inaccurate. All art is temporal. As a creative activity and product, art reflects its history, the available techniques, the artist's skill, and the varying receptivity of audiences. As a kind of experience, the perception of art, even of the so-called spatial arts like painting and sculpture, transpires in time and requires duration to develop in awareness and to work on the perceiver.[77] Failing to acknowledge this is yet another consequence of the mistaken concentration on the art object rather

---

[76] It should be clear that it is *aesthetic perception* that I am calling intrinsic, not *aesthetic value*. The following chapter will probe into the question of aesthetic value, and will develop the view that aesthetic value is both intrinsic and instrumental, thus differentiating itself in this analysis from the perceptual experience of art.

[77] "A work of art is a tightly-knit system of reciprocal influences and qualifications. The 'things' in it are what they are because of their interrelations with everything else, which extend throughout the work. They can be known for what they are only if, as the work unfolds in time, we 'go beyond what we are at the moment noticing.'" J. Stolnitz, "Some Questions concerning Aesthetic Perception," *Philosophy and Phenomenological Research*, XXII (Sept. 1961), p. 86.

than on the experiential situation in which it is a factor.

Yet not only is timelessness perceptually inaccurate; it is honorifically inappropriate as well. The art object is not an independent thing. It rather acquires its significance and its very sustenance from its ability to function effectively in the aesthetic field. And this ability, too, is conditioned by the historical needs of particular societies. Art, even the very best art, is always going out of fashion and coming back into fashion. Thus in both our perceptual experience and our social valuings, timelessness misrepresents art's intrinsic quality.

The same intrinsic quality of aesthetic perception may explain the popularity of such notions as isolation and disinterestedness in discussions of the aesthetic attitude. Taken in and for itself, the experience of art need not rest upon its consequences for justification; it does not function as a means to an end that stretches beyond itself. Hence the attitude toward art appears to differ from the characteristic attitude we take toward objects of practical life. We try to facilitate our observance of this difference by isolating the art object and assuming an attitude in which we regard experience with the art object in clear isolation from surrounding and ever-impinging practical influences. Bullough's theory of psychical distance, Ortega's concept of dehumanization, and Lange's use of the notion of art as play involving conscious self-deception all become understandable in part, not, as we have seen, as accurate descriptions of the appreciative attitude, but as expressions of the intrinsic perception that occurs in aesthetic experience. By somehow disengaging ourselves from the art object, by erecting a barrier of psychological distance and yet retaining a tenuous connection with it, we are led to approach art differently from the way in which we come to our other experiences. We enjoy the activity of aesthetic perception for itself, judging it by its own standards and in its own realm. It is not a substitute either for other experiences or other things, something which theories that attempt to explain art as a kind of imitation or as illusion fail to recognize. Despite its overstatement, the romantic insistence on *art pour l'art* was a call to accept the intrinsic perceptual claim of art. As a legitimate area of human activity, art must be adjudged by independent criteria, and to do this it must be perceived in and for itself.[78]

These ideas all try to render aesthetic experience distinct from the involvement in a matrix of transitory means and ends by which one is bound up in practical experience, distracted from the qualitative nature of the world around us. Yet in attempting to keep the experience of art separate from the pulls and pushes of practical activity, these proposals, as we have seen, tend to place the experiencer in a distant seat where he becomes more than disinterested; he is left remote, detached, and uninvolved. The immediacy of our resonse is discouraged and may vanish altogether.

Thus in trying to avoid one error, another is committed. We strive to render aesthetic perception possible by removing the art object from its practical setting and placing it on a stage under a proscenium arch, putting a frame around it or setting it on a pedestal and placing it in an impersonal gallery away from pressing activities, or performing it in a hall reserved exclusively for that purpose. These are attempts to create a situation in which the mediate function of normal, practical experience is neither demanded nor expected, a setting in which it is conventionally acceptable to drop the expectant attitude of practical perception and to participate directly in the intrinsic perception of sensory stimuli. However, in attempting to avoid the practical, we often cut off aesthetic experience from conditions which encourage an immediate response to its intrinsic qualities and promote, instead, the contemplative (and unaesthetic) responses of disengagement and deliberation.

Here, then, is a matter of paramount importance for an accurate understanding of aesthetic experience. It is the recognition that the perception of art must be taken on its own terms as intrinsic perception. Furthermore, if we insist on separating aesthetic perception from the network of causal

---

[78] . . . (E)sthetic experience is experience in its integrity. . . . Esthetic experience is pure experience. For it is experience freed from the forces that impede and confuse its development as experience; freed, that is, from factors that subordinate an experience as it is directly had to something beyond itself." John Dewey, *Art as Experience* (New York, Minton, Balch, 1934), p. 274.

action and practical purpose, we are led to consider by this standard for perception all experience in which we engage in and for its own sake. Experience is the whole of human life. Aesthetic experience is experience that is had for itself, and all intrinsic experience is, to that extent, aesthetic. This, perhaps, is what Whitehead meant when he described each individual act of immediate self-enjoyment as an "occasion of experience" and called such acts "the only really real things."

In this fashion we can transcend the traditional limits of art by a perceptual route that bypasses the practical without confining the aesthetic. Instead of either adopting the restrictive notions of isolation and disengagement or relinquishing art to practical uses, it becomes possible both to retain the self-sufficiency of aesthetic experience and to allow it universal scope.

Integral

Aesthetic theory has often been identified with questions of form. Principles of unity, of order, of harmony and cohesion have frequently dominated discussions of art since the earliest beginnings of aesthetic thought. Sometimes form is contrasted favorably with matter; at other times it is opposed to content or idea. Entire theories have been developed in which formal factors are the primary ones. For Plato, Aristotle, and Plotinus, form was associated with the intellectual, contemplative ideal, although in significantly different ways. Form was the chief cause of beauty for St. Augustine and St. Thomas, and they were followed in this by all the middle ages. Modern aesthetics is no exception, and it, too, has given emphasis to the role of form. Cassirer elaborated the concept of symbolic form, Bell and Fry stressed the notion of significant form, Langer has combined the concept of significant form with presentational symbol, and Arnheim has applied Gestalt psychology to the visual perception of shape, pattern and form. These and others have ridden the leading wave of a tradition that often combined insights into our aesthetic awareness with confusions in aesthetic theory.

Form has been the main appeal in the effort to elevate art to a status that leaves it independent of changes in style, taste, culture, and history, and this effort has covered a wide range. Attempts have been made to give art a kind of ideal existence, standing in pure and immortal splendor. The assertion that great art has an eternal nature, both in the sense of being lasting in significance and timeless in effect, is largely the outcome of an intellectual emphasis on the formal aspects of art. Form, aesthetically as well as ontologically, has traditionally been regarded as the stable aspect of things, imposing an identity largely independent of the particular materials which fill it out. Yet this high regard for order and structure is largely the result of an object-centered, rationalistic aesthetics. It is a clear expression of the persistent but misdirected effort to elevate art on intellectual standards by eternalizing it, and to interpret rationally as timeless what is intrinsically experiential and thus temporal. There have also been more modest efforts to overcome the subjectivity of our response by endowing art with a stability and objectivity that would allow it to retain an authority of its own, and this has often taken expression as an emphasis on form. Finally there has been the endeavor to approach the art object as something that is self-contained and self-sufficient and to which we must adapt our appreciative response and our critical demands, again by stressing its formal features.

Perhaps the main problem in a discussion of artistic form lies in a fundamental confusion that frequently occurs between what we might call *analytic form,* the formal character of objects, and *perceptual form,* the formal qualities of perceptual experience. Seldom are these distinguished clearly and consistently. When the treatment of form does not confine itself entirely to analytic form, it either wavers between analysis and perception or assumes a dualism of perceiver and object in which the formal nature of the art object imposes a certain restraint or order upon our perception of it. Let us consider some typical cases.

Both D. W. Gotshalk and DeWitt H. Parker have written with considerable awareness on the subject of artistic form, but like many they have confined their treatment to the formal character of art objects. Gotshalk, for example, identifies four principles of artistic form that serve to increase the object's intrinsic perceptual interest: harmony, balance, centrality, and development. Out of these he derives others such as rhythm, measure, hierarchy, and dominance.[79] Despite the etymology of the term "aesthetic," Parker analyzes the logic of "esthetic form" by enumerating principles that refer to the art object: the principle of organic unity, the principle of the theme, the principle of thematic variation, balance, the principle of hierarchy, and evolution.[80] While these accounts of analytic form unquestionably serve a valuable purpose, they are clearly limited, for they restrict themselves to the formal boundaries of the art object with hardly a glance at the aesthetic field in which it is a functioning part.

When Bell and Fry speak of significant form, a definite connection is drawn between the formal characteristics of the object and our appreciative response to it. Form they take to be the relations and design constituted in particular out of the pictorial elements of the fine arts. (Although their views originated from the practice of art criticism, these were not and need not be restricted to the fine arts.) When we confine our attention to mass, color, line, and composition and exclude recognition of whatever may be represented and of the associations that it evokes, a coordinate feeling arises—the aesthetic emotion. Thus form is restricted to art objects, although it is connected with the feeling of the observer.[81]

Arnheim finds a similar relationship between the object and our experience of it: "In the great works of art the deepest significance is transmitted to the eye with powerful directness by the perceptual characteristics of the compositional pattern."[82] Langer, too, sees forms in art as abstracted objects which carry on an exchange with the sensitive perceiver by acting as symbols of human feeling. At times, as when she speaks of "living form," the two seem to come close together, with form exhibiting the biological activities of growth and decay. Yet the art object

---

[79] *Art and the Social Order*, 2nd ed. (New York, Dover, 1962), Ch. V.

[80] *The Analysis of Art* (New Haven, Yale University Press, 1926), Ch. II.

[81] Roger Fry, *The Hogarth Papers*, in M. Rader, ed., *A Modern Book of Esthetics*, 3rd ed., pp. 304-309.

[82] *Art and Visual Perception*, p. 436.

retains its separate identity and remains an expressive form.[83] Cassirer comes closer to merging analytic and perceptual form. Art, for him, is a realm of symbolic form from which we gain the intuition of the form of things. Yet the dynamic process of life that art expresses is not wholly separate from us. For Cassirer, aesthetic intuition overcomes the division between the objective and the subjective worlds. Living forms emerge, and the aesthetic experience consists in our absorption in their dynamic aspect.[84]

Now the obvious may well be merely the customary, and it would be wise occasionally to look beyond it. For us to take issue with the analytic treatment of form may resemble arguing that the world is flat. Yet it would be well to remember that while the earth is not flat, it appears to be so in our perception of it. If, therefore, our purpose were to elucidate perceptual experience, we would err in being content with a geodesic account. So, too, with art. To maintain that form is a property of the object is to claim a truth, to be sure, but a partial one. If art cannot be disentangled from its participation in a mode of experience without irreversibly distorting our conception of it, how then can we expect to provide an adequate treatment of form unless we expand our scope of vision to encompass the full range of aesthetic perception?

This of course is not an entirely new proposal, and aestheticians have often found themselves groping in this direction. Too often, though, they have been hindered by the illusory ease of a traditional entry into the problem of form. Parker, for example, has given us a valuable hint in observing that "unity of a work of art is the counterpart of a unity within the experience of the beholder."[85] Yet he is hampered by the old, deep gulf between the object and perceiver of art that has somehow to be bridged. Stolnitz, too, is sensitive to the perceptual role of form in the art object, yet in spite of his concern for its perceptual function,

---

[83] Suzanne K. Langer, *Feeling and Form*, Chs. 3 and 4; *Problems of Art* (New York, Scribner's, 1957), pp. 52-54.

[84] Ernst Cassirer, *An Essay on Man*, pp. 184-194.

[85] *The Analysis of Art*, p. 35.

he joins Parker in identifying form as a characteristic of the object.

Form, Stolnitz claims, has three functions. First, it directs the attention of the spectator toward certain elements in the work,[86] so that we are able to distinguish a climax from a transition, repetition from contrast. Form here, we should notice, performs a cognitive activity, and one that has a didactic function. It works to discriminate, to identify different parts of an art object, and to guide us in recognizing them. A second function of form lies in arranging the elements that make up the object so that their expressive and sensory values emerge more clearly.[87] This is a more straightforward perceptual function, one that resembles Parker's comment on unity. Here the arrangement of formal elements in the object corresponds with the expressive and sensory topography of our perception of it. The final aesthetic function of form lies in its intrinsic aesthetic value.[88] With this function we approach the merging of object and perception, although this is obscured by assigning form a kind of value. It seems to identify an evaluative function rather than an experiential one, confounding the way in which formal features of the art object function in our appreciative attention with a judgment of the value of that function. Yet despite the questions one can raise, Stolnitz's discussion of the perceptual functions of form is a sensitive and valuable one.

Yet the attempt to move beyond the limitations of the object may lead to the other extreme, confining order entirely to the psychology of the observer. This is the difficulty with the analysis of the aesthetic experience of beauty that Ogden, Richards, and Wood have made. The aesthetic state in which we experience beauty they term "synaesthesis," and it is characterized by equilibrium and harmony. Order there is, to be sure, yet the harmony which synaesthesis possesses results from the inter-relation and coordination of impulses, and the entire experience is analyzed exclusively as psychological.[89]

---

[86] *Aesthetics and Philosophy of Art Criticism*, pp. 236-239.
[87] *Ibid.*, pp. 239-242.
[88] *Ibid.*, pp. 242-244.
[89] *The Foundations of Aesthetics* (New York, 1922).

Dewey's treatment of artistic form comes closest to what we have been searching for. "Form," he states, "is a character of every experience that is *an* experience."[90] It is in the arts that the conditions for achieving unity of experience are most deliberately and fully realized. Thus Dewey defines form as "the operation of forces that carry the experience of an event, object, scene and situation to its own integral fulfillment." Further, he proceeds to resolve the dichotomy between object and experience by asserting that "the connection of form with substance is thus inherent, not imposed from without. It marks the matter of an experience that is carried to consummation."[91] What is most exceptional about Dewey's treatment of form is his constant awareness of the perceptual unity into which the beholder and object of art combine during aesthetic experience. "When the structure of the object is such that its force interacts happily (but not easily) with the energies that issue from the experience itself; when their mutual affinities and antagonisms work together to bring about a substance that develops cumulatively and surely (but not too steadily) toward a fulfilling of impulsions and tensions, then indeed there is a work of art. . . . But an esthetic experience, the work of art in its actuality, is *perception*."[92]

It is through his notion of "*an* experience" that Dewey calls attention to the order and integrity of the aesthetic event. In contrast to the disarray of the mechanical routine in which we ordinarily experience our world, aesthetic experience has a cohesion in which the material we experience "runs its course to fulfillment."[93] This is the source of the indivisibility that has so often been ascribed to the work of art. Far from being the analytic unity of an object, it is rather, as Croce held, activity that is a "fusion of the impressions in an organic whole."[94] Order, in its aesthetic sense, Dewey maintained, "is defined and measured by functional and operative traits."[95] Moreover, the

---

[90] *Art as Experience*, p. 137.
[91] *Loc. cit.*
[92] *Ibid.*, p. 162.
[93] *Ibid.*, p. 35.
[94] *Aesthetic*, p. 20.
[95] *Art as Experience*, p. 65.

binding force that unites the elements of aesthetic experience is its qualitativeness, and the qualitativeness of aesthetic experience is the quality of a whole. In some ways this feature is identical with the mode of aesthetic experience itself, becoming the dimension of the aesthetic field as we encounter it in our experience. Here quality comes to constitute and delimit the aesthetic situation, and the pervasiveness of aesthetic quality is the unifying force.[96]

Thus a synthesis of a sort appears to emerge in a way that recalls Cassirer's claim that aesthetic intuition overcomes the division between the objective and subjective worlds. As primary perception, our engagement with art is a mode of experience that resembles the primitive or childlike. Heinz Werner has termed this the "mode of magic," in which phenomena that appear separate, clear, and discrete to a critical mind merge instead into a diffuse whole.[97] Yet instead of overcoming the separateness of phenomena and the division of the world into what is subjective and what objective, this unity of aesthetic experience precedes that division. In fact this unity is the best evidence for the artificiality of the dualisms between mind and body, subject and object, that have plagued aesthetic thinking. Not only are these distinctions inapplicable to such experience; if applied in our encounter with art, they inhibit or even prevent that experience from fulfilling itself.[98] Aesthetic experience transcends psychophysical and epistemological dualisms, for it is the condition of an engagement of perceiver and object in a unified relationship that is forcefully immediate and direct.

Here is the lead we have been seeking. Instead of a frag-

---

[96] Cf. John Dewey's highly perceptive discussion in "Qualitative Thought," *Philosophy and Civilization* (New York, 1931), pp. 93-116, 97-99, 114, esp. 93, 96. Cf. also J. H. Randall, Jr., *Nature and Historical Experience* (New York, Columbia University Press, 1958), Ch. 10.

[97] *Comparative Psychology of Mental Development*, pp. 67-82, Cf. also M. Lipman, *What Happens in Art*, p. 57.

[98] "The [Cartesian dualistic] model leaves only one way to take a really objective look at things, namely, the perception that qualifies as observation; and this must be under controls that eventually purge it even of sensations or sensory impressions, as well as of feelings, if the point is to take the most knowing look at things. Thus is perception dissipated in favor of conception or thought." Virgil Aldrich, *Philosophy of Art*, p. 9.

mented concatenation of independent elements, the aesthetic field reveals a perceptual order and unity. Thus we can properly describe aesthetic experience as integral. It is experience which achieves its own unity when its boundaries can be defined functionally by the way in which the appreciator and the art object combine with the other factors in the aesthetic field to form a unified perceptual environment, an experiential totality.[99] Only as it functions perceptually, then, can we identify the limits and reveal the cohesion of any art object.

In *Vision and Design* Roger Fry has illustrated how unity in the pictorial arts may become a unity of experience. When we look at certain Chinese painted silk scrolls, we can see them only in successive segments, rolling the scroll up at one end as we unroll it at the other. As we do this, "we traverse wide stretches of country, tracing, perhaps, all the vicissitudes of a river from its source to the sea, and yet, when this is well done, we have received a very keen impression of pictorial unity." This kind of unity "depends upon the forms being presented to us in such a sequence that each successive element is felt to have a fundamental and harmonious relation with that which preceded it. I suggest that in looking at drawings our sense of pictorial unity is largely of this nature; we feel, if the drawing be a good one, that each modulation of the line as our eye passes along it gives order and variety to our sensations. Such a drawing may be almost entirely lacking in the geometrical balance which we are accustomed to demand in paintings, and yet have, in a remarkable degree, unity."

Not only can we regard pictorial unity in experiential terms; we can do the same with the other arts. Take the case of music. Because music is directly and immediately perceptual without a physical object to distract and absorb our attention, it raises the insistent demand to be taken on its own terms as experience. Moreover, music sharpens for us the differences between the ways in which art is experienced and the ways in which those experiences are understood and conceptualized. Yet it is none-theless common to treat the musical object in conceptual terms

---

[99] "The aesthetic character of an act or of an object is its function of totality, its existence both subjective and objective as a remarkable point." Simondon.

rather than perceptual ones, substituting analytic form for perceptual form.

Consider, for example, the problem of what constitutes a piece of music.[100] The question has been raised about whether multi-movement works, such as a symphony, a suite, or an introit of a mass that contains a trope, are single musical pieces or collections of pieces. Is a four-movement symphony four pieces or one, a six-movement suite six individual compositions or one, or the three separate sections of a trope that has been interpolated into an introit three pieces or a single one? Questions have also been asked about whether one ought more properly to treat music as process or as object. Is Edgar Varèse's *Ionization,* a work whose closely knit formal organization enables the listener to remove himself from what is going on by stepping back and interposing "distance" between himself and the piece, more successfully identified as a piece of music than John Cage's *Variations for Orchestra and Dance,* a work which demands the participation of the perceiver in a flow of organized sound? Some writers have opted in favor of an objectively analyzable formal structure, so that our awareness of form carries us beyond the constant motion of the musical process to the contemplation from a distance of the object as a whole.

Now we can all recognize a vast range in degrees of formal coherence. What is at issue, however, is the extent to which formal integrity is necessary for music to become an object, and, even more basic and important, what the nature of such form is and how it can best be described. The first question is largely empirical. The kind of coherence that is relevant to a discussion of music is primarily auditory, and it is the light of its experiential (and not its analytical) orderliness that we must appraise it. Performance practices, for example, may have a decisive influence on the perceptual integrity of a musical work. Whether there are lengthy interruptions as for applause within or between movements, whether the movements are performed individually, whether they are interspersed with arias and other totally

_____

[100] The following discussion is taken in large part from my paper, "Music as Sound and Idea," *Current Musicology,* No. 6, 1968, pp. 95-100, and is used with the kind permission of the editor.

unrelated works of other composers as was the custom at one time, such conditions for perception exercise a profound influence on whether or not such works are perceived as a unity. Moreover, it is possible that the Cage *Variations* possesses minimal aural coherence sufficient to be fairly regarded as a musical piece, and that the participation of the perceiver in the musical flow makes possible a greater unity of experience than distancing ever could. Furthermore, our willingness to take certain through-composed songs of, say, Schubert and Debussy as pieces suggests that tight structural organization is not essential for auditory coherence. Stylistic congruity may be enough. In addition, the use of chance techniques that has become increasingly common in the contemporary arts may itself provide a measure of freshness and spontaneity that will hold our attention and, perhaps, provide a measure of order by imposing the demand for organizing the experience on the perceiver instead of exclusively on the artist. As long as it is the *perceptual form* that we are concerned with and not analytic form, our answers lie in the region of the psychology and sociology of aesthetic perception.

Music, then, comes first and foremost as experience. Indeed, in certain respects it epitomizes the perceptual qualities of all art, for in comparison with other artistic media the musical experience is less fraught with those resemblances, relationships, and associations which distract and mislead us. These, unfortunately, create problems for an aesthetic of the visual arts, and produce difficulties which are particularly grave in the case of the literary ones.

In the directness of our experience, music appears as a phenomenal object. Here it is a perceptually congruent grouping of sounds, silences, and secondary visual, kinesthetic, and other active-passive sensory events. In this form, music is grasped in its intuitive experiential immediacy. When we proceed to describe and understand musical experience, we can employ broad *perceptual categories* such as sound and motion, or more specific ones such as pitch, duration, timbre, dynamics, tonal succession, and juxtaposition. These categories are the musical concepts with which the composer works. However, music may also be described in *conceptual* or *analytic* categories like sonata-allegro form, harmonic rhythm, thematic relationships, style, and so forth. These are the concepts that the musicologist and theorist use in analyzing a musical work. It is certainly true that the perceptual and conceptual categories can and do overlap, yet the difference between them lies in the primary reference either to immediate auditory-experiential qualities or to the activities of analysis and organization. These categories resemble one another, however, in that they are comprised of referential symbols that are conceived apart from the actual perception of music and that depend on language rather than on sound. Their source and the touchstone of their validity, however, remain the musical experience.

The composer occupies an ambiguous position. As a worker in musical materials he operates in the phenomenal medium of musical perception; yet when he pauses to reflect on or to explain what he is doing, he shifts to perceptual (and occasionally to conceptual) categories. Still, there is a striking consistency in the testimony of creative artists about their reliance on purely perceptual qualities in making creative decisions. They simply "like it that way" because "it sounds better."

There is, I believe, a good deal of evidence that favors the adoption of this distinction in the musical object between the experiential and the categorical, the perceptual and the analytic. The history of music abounds with examples of ingenious technical bravado incorporated into a musical work which simply do not succeed in performance. And we all recognize how the aural integrity of a musical piece need not necessarily correspond with a unity that can be discovered by analyzing it. If we wish, then, to be clear about what a musical piece is, we must recognize that it achieves its identity and its formal integrity as a perceptual object.

The same considerations that I have applied to the question of artistic form can be directed toward an issue that has come in for a good deal of discussion in recent years, the problem of the definition of art.[101] The difficulty in circumscribing the

----

[101] Cf. A. Berleant, "A Note on the Problem of Defining 'Art,'" *Philosophy and Phenomenological Research*, XXV, 2 (Dec. 1964), 239-241. Reprinted in H. G. Duffield, *Problems in Criticism of the Arts* (San Francisco, Chandler, 1968), pp. 240-242.

limits of art, of setting it off from the nonaesthetic, exactly corresponds on a level of greater generality to the form of a musical or other artistic work. If the definition of art is taken exclusively as a conceptual, analytic problem, independent of the activity of the arts, the discussion dissipates into interminable wrangling that ends with claims for its very impossibility. We cannot successfully define art, however, by confining ourselves to the objects which the term denotes. The limits of art are not the limits of objects taken in isolation but rather of objects as they function in perception. And the object functions in a situation which has its own internal coherence and whose boundaries are determinate enough to allow us to set it off from the experience which surrounds it. The problem of defining art thus is transformed into the problem of demarcating the boundaries of aesthetic experience. Instead of the analytic grouping of *objects* we now have a perceptual criterion for identifying *situations*. And the formal features of the object become explicable as tensions which define the structure of aesthetic experience.[102] The formal integrity of art exists then in perception alone. "Art," Conrad Fiedler wrote in his richly suggestive book, *On Judging Works of Visual Art*, "has nothing to do with forms that are found ready-made prior to its activity and independent of it. Rather, the beginning and the end of artistic activity reside in the creation of forms which only thereby attain existence. Art does not start from abstract thought in order to arrive at forms; rather, it climbs up from the formless to the formed. . . ."[103]

Finally, the integrity of aesthetic experience is, at its fullest and most complete, a social experience. Aesthetic experience is not the last residue of privacy, of subjectivity, of human isolation. On the contrary, it is a common experience which transpires in a social situation and becomes the experience of full community. It is the string quartet in which each instrument is essential yet needing the equal partnership and subtle responsiveness of the others to create a unified musical experience. It is the

---

[102] Cf. S. Langer, "Abstraction in Art," *J. of Aesthetics and Art Criticism*, XXII, 4 (Summer 1964), pp. 381 ff.

[103] (Berkeley and Los Angeles, University of California Press, 1957), pp. 48-49.

religious experience of the medieval cathedral, truly a multi-media total sensory environment, fusing architecture, sculpture in the round and in relief; pictorial art in murals, stained glass, and painting; drama, literature, and music in the liturgy; and even involving taste and smell in the wine, the wafer, and incense.[104] It is the goal of humanistic community planning. These along with many others epitomize the aesthetic integrity of social experience.

This, however, is not a return to what Jung called "the state of *participation mystique*," in which the individual is caught up and loses his identity in "man," and in which his own fate does not matter but only that of human existence. Aesthetic experience is, rather, an integral part of primary experience, and thus an experience of social integration that reaffirms the original unity of men in human society. As Mikel Dufrenne once commented,[105] in our present state of civilization aesthetic experience is all that is left to exemplify the original harmony between man and world.[106]

AESTHETIC EXPERIENCE AND AESTHETIC THEORY

This account of aesthetic experience is an analytic portrayal of what is perceptually unified and continuous. Experience itself possesses no sharp separations. Thus the distinctions that I have drawn result from the *analysis* of experience and from the contrast between aesthetic theory and the experience it must clarify. This does not lead to perceptual divisions but rather to

---

[104] Cf. Edward T. Cone, "What is a Composition," *Current Musicology* No. 5 (1967), pp. 106-107. This account of medieval cathedral suggests Harold Taylor's characterization of the fair as the art of the future.

[105] In a lecture given at the University of Buffalo, September, 1960.

[106] "In art as an experience, actuality and possibility or ideality, the new and the old, objective material and personal response, the individual and the universal, surface and depth, sense and meaning, are integrated in an experience in which they are all transfigured from the significance that belongs to them when isolated in reflection. 'Nature,' said Goethe, 'has neither kernel nor shell.' Only in esthetic experience is this statement completely true. Of art as experience it is also true that nature has neither subjective nor objective being; is neither individual nor universal, sensuous nor rational. The significance of art as experience is, therefore, incomparable for the adventure of philosophic thought." John Dewey, *Art as Experience*, p. 297.

conceptual discriminations. Thus one must be careful to distinguish between the aesthetic field which regards aesthetic experience in general terms on an analytic, reflective level, and the aesthetic transaction which is the particular occurrence of aesthetic experience on the experiential level. The first is cognitive, the second noncognitive. The same distinction carries over, as we shall see in the following chapter, to the discrimination between aesthetic perception and art criticism and between aesthetic valuing and evaluation. To exclude the cognitive from aesthetic experience is far from embracing anti-intellectualism in aesthetics. It is rather the result of an effort to chart the geography of experience without confounding the map with the topography it schematizes and without confusing land with sea.

Such an approach to aesthetics provides the basis for a matrix definition of aesthetic experience. While the proposal that this chapter makes is provisional and incomplete, it is nevertheless not an arbitrary one. By grounding itself descriptively on a literal account of the aesthetic field, this portrayal of aesthetic experience avoids surrogates and faces common data directly and with candor. Thus it suggests a great many directions for investigation in the behavioral sciences in the search for a stable body of aesthetic facts on which to ground theory successfully. We need to make many specific studies of particular objects in the different arts to discover the characteristic ways in which they function in the aesthetic field. What are the features of poetic experience, musical experience, theatrical, sculptural, architectural, filmic experiences? Such questions as these cannot be answered without a careful examination of the aesthetic dimensions of each artistic mode, and this requires us to explore specific instances of each. Too often we are presented with disconnected studies of particular works on the one hand, and with general pronouncements on the other. To be significant and to achieve theoretical backing and force, we must join both the specific critical examinations and the theoretical generalizations under the unifying aegis of a comprehensive account. In the same fashion we must bring the psychology and sociology of aesthetic perception to bear on the perceiver's function in the aesthetic field, and explore in detail how particular biological, psychological, technological, historical, and cultural factors influence the experiential qualities of the field. The development of a scientifically grounded aesthetics cannot therefore be the achievement of a single investigator but rather the cumulative product of collective inquiry. It would help but little to avoid the cul-de-sac of the surrogate theories only to fall into the pit of presumption.

V

ART CRITICISM AND AESTHETIC VALUE

W HEN PEOPLE DISCUSS art, it is usually not long before conversation fails. We may talk with at least a show of communication and even with occasional agreement as long as we speak
about the traits of an art object—its stylistic features, historical
position, formal analysis, and even at times its interpretative
explanations. For in each of these cases there is a common point
of reference that everyone must acknowledge—the art object
itself. Remove the painting, poem, or prelude, and the words are
left suspended in mid-air with no place on which to alight.

But when the topic turns to the judgment of art, the situation
is changed. Here everyone seems able to make appraisals of
equal authority, and disagreements, reduced to irreconcilable
differences in taste, remain unresolved. No longer does conversation have the same referent. There is rather what appears to
be a final and irredeemable basis for disagreement—the exclusively private sensibilities of the appreciator. Some may take
comfort in such a haven for free and independent judgment.
Yet one can regard the apparent impossibility of critical agreement as an unfortunate structural barrier to the growth of
knowledge, and as a lonely and unsatisfactory refuge for
embattled sensibilities.

This state of affairs, however, is not as bleak and disheartening
(or, to some, as safe and secure) as it might seem. If instead
of removing the criticism of art from the realm of aesthetic
activity and considering it in isolation, we turned rather to the
world of art to see how critical judgment actually operates in
our dealings with art, we would find that these conclusions
become somewhat more questionable and, indeed, refutable. By
examining the actual conduct of criticism and the context in

159

which it occurs, we may discover that an alternative route to the judgment of art will emerge.

Critics are what critics do. What better way to clarify the function of criticism in art than to examine the practices of the critics themselves? What do they talk about? What do they intend to accomplish? How do they proceed? But more important than these, exactly what role do critics and criticism play in the world of artistic activity?

CONVENTIONAL FUNCTIONS OF CRITICISM

Typically, critics are expected to determine the aesthetic merits of an art object or performance, and they approach this in a variety of ways. To support their judgments, they may offer information which they obtain by examining features in the art object: How effectively are the characters developed, how credible are their actions, how fresh and evocative is the linguistic imagery, how rich are the thematic materials, and how competently are they developed? How skillful is the use of line, the handling of color, the arrangement of compositional elements? And again, how are sounds handled, how are the melodic motives treated, how tight is the musical structure and how smoothly do the materials unfold? Or critics may note the personal or cultural circumstances that attend the creation of the art object: Does the work exhibit technical innovations? By whom was the artist influenced? What were his intentions and how well did he succeed in realizing them? How effectively does his work reveal his personality or his milieu? Further, the critic may cite standards that are currently deemed authoritative: Does the work display formal unity, does it debase the person who perceives it, is it highly original, does it contribute toward achieving particular social goals? And finally, how exciting is the work? Does it evoke a pleasurable emotional response? Does it capture the interest or imagination? In the case of the performing arts, there are analogous questions: How skillful is the execution? How true is the performance to the style and character of the work or its creator? What is its effect on the audience or on the critic? These and many others are the sorts of issues typically raised, and all seem to have the same purpose—to come to some conclusion about the merits of an art object or an artistic performance.

All this suggests the conventional view that critics are properly judges of artistic merit. When they act responsibly, they base their evaluations on full experience, sufficient knowledge, and a developed aesthetic sensibility. Yet the abuses often laid at the doorstep of critics are more than shortcomings of experience, knowledge, and sensibility. They are often directed toward a misuse of the critical function. "People criticize a picture by their ear," complained an ancient Chinese critic-painter in the *Book of Tea*. Sometimes, however, the fault lies not with irrelevancy but with confusion of roles, as when the literary critic competes with the author by writing parasitic poetry of his own, waxing eloquent over the corpus of the artist, as wolves will howl over their fallen prey. Then there are those critics who remove themselves far from the backstage mechanics of artistic production, declaiming their pronouncements with philosophic authority from their box seat at a metaphysical theater. In any case, whether the critic acts responsibly or not, we continue to regard his role as that of an aesthetic arbiter.

In contrast with these conventional functions of criticism, I should like to propose something rather different. It is to suggest that the critic's main contribution lies in *educating* his readers to the reasons for the success or failure of the art object rather than in deciding on its merit. And further, I want to suggest that artistic success or failure is measured by the effectiveness with which the art object or performance *works* in the aesthetic field and therefore contributes to our aesthetic experience. If this is so, then the critical evaluation of any art object is actually the long-range response of the artistic public. That is to say, the critic's role does not lie so much in his particular appraisal of an art object; his main contribution comes from an ability to transmit the aesthetic perception on which his judgment rests. In doing this he adds to the store of common experience of the object, and it is such experience which eventually leads to a relatively stable critical appraisal. The critic's observations, then, are part of the body of expert commentary, and all commentators are, to that extent, critics. Together with the rest of the artistic public, they develop a conflux of common evaluative knowledge, which in turn bears its fruit in the social experience of art.

THE CRITICAL OBJECT

The direction which an account of criticism will take clearly depends upon whatever is regarded as its proper object. Alternative theories of art criticism emerge as one expects it to be directed either toward the art object, toward the creative origins of the art object, or toward the appreciative response it evokes. Each of these critical approaches rests, however, on a fragmented view of aesthetic experience. Each grasps at a single aspect of the setting in which art occurs, and in so doing arrives at an unavoidably incomplete judgment. Object-centered criticism is likely to be unduly rationalistic, for in focusing attention on the art object, we are likely to neglect its function in perception. The critic occupies himself primarily with the structure, form, style, or content of the object, and has little time or inclination to direct his attention elsewhere. Psychological or genetic criticism, on the other hand, is prone to ignore the aesthetic priority of the finished work by its concern with the motives or biography of the artist. And criticism directed by the observer's response is frequently disposed to slight the structural and qualitative features of the object in favor of its emotional effects on the perceiver.

If we are to avoid distorting our explanation of the place of criticism by giving only a fragmentary account, we must interpret the critical activity differently. We must regard criticism as actually directed toward the full setting in which art functions, rather than being concerned with only a single aspect of it. Because art objects are things to be experienced, and because the explanation and criticism of the experiences associated with them must take the function of the objects into account, it is necessary to look at the total context in which we experience art. This setting in which art is experienced is, as we have seen, the aesthetic field, and it is this field which is the proper concern of critics. While Chapter III developed the concept of the aesthetic field in some detail, it will help to examine it once more in order to see how it acts as the proper object of criticism.

In describing the aesthetic field, it is unwise to regard its structure rigidly. Precisely because aesthetic experience takes place in a fluid yet cohesive setting, reducing the aesthetic field analytically into its component parts will invariably distort it. Still, it is possible to locate several factors that operate in the field, and it is these that have been the loci of the various traditional theories of criticism. There is the art object—a painting, a musical performance, or a novel, for instance—which participates in the aesthetic field. It contains a variety of material features such as color, sound, movement, mass, light, and language. These features, of course, are capable of fine degrees of differentiation. Color, for example, may be analyzed into hue, value, and intensity, and it exercises an influence in composition through quantity, arrangement, and the like. Similar distinctions may be made of the formal, stylistic, and other dimensions of art objects. Furthermore, art objects cannot be regarded in isolation; they are part of a history and a tradition, and each may share with other art objects the influence of similar materials and techniques. Because such objects are perceived substantially alike by most observers, it is possible to achieve a considerable measure of stability and agreement in aesthetic evaluation, but more of this later.

Then there is the object's appreciator. More than a passive observer, the aesthetic perceiver engages the object. The association between them is not that of independent things interacting with one another; rather it is a kind of transactional relationship in which perceiver and perceived are functionally inseparable, each becoming what it is by its intimate dependence on the other. The place of the artist in the aesthetic field, moreover, closely parallels that of the perceiver, from which it differs more in degree than in kind.

Yet the art appreciator cannot be taken as a singular individual. He does not sit alone and aloof. Actually he is a participant in a community of perceivers. This is often directly the case when art is experienced in the company of an audience, performers, and other seemingly unconnected perceivers. Yet it is equally the case indirectly, for one brings to his perception of art the conditioning, training, and expectations which he has acquired from his social and cultural experiences. These include his past acquaintance with art, his likings, and his biases. They include, too, the cultural traditions he has inherited and the very art forms and media available to him, along with the history of art, and its techniques and equipment. The participation of society appears, as well, through the means it provides such as theaters, galleries, and concert halls. Such common cultural influences combine with common biological and psychological traits to function as a fairly stable base for perception, while at the same time allowing for differences which account for the variability in perception and response that exists. To the extent that perceivers of art possess these features in common with one another, their perception and judgments will have a high degree of resemblance. And to the extent that these factors differ, degrees of variability are introduced, ranging from individual variations that result from diversities in training and experience, physical endowment, and attitudes, to culturally induced differences in response. All these elements and influences combine to form the context in which experience of art occurs. Figure 4 offers a partial iconographic representation of this description of the aesthetic field.

A theory of criticism is adequate only to the extent that it is able to account for the relevant data of the experience and criticism of art. Among the more significant data are the broad range of perceptual and critical agreement, and the sorts of circumstances under which disagreement on aesthetic effectiveness and judgment typically seem to occur. The concept of the aesthetic field provides the basis for a more satisfactory explanation of the data of critical agreement and dispute than one can achieve by introducing objective principles or standards external to aesthetic experience, or by invoking the unavoidable subjectivity of our aesthetic responses. Further, an examination of the aesthetic field can also help illuminate the role that the critic plays in the world of art. For in relation to this field, the able critic acts not just as a perceiver whose training and experience unite with natural endowments to permit a full and

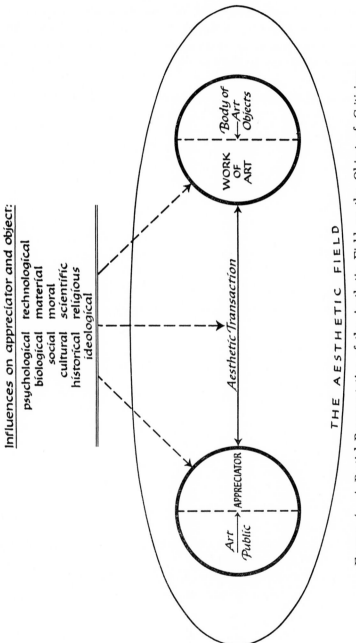

Influences on appreciator and object:

psychological technological
biological material
social moral
cultural scientific
historical religious
ideological

Aesthetic Transaction

WORK
OF
ART

*Body of
Art
Objects*

APPRECIATOR

*Art
Public*

THE AESTHETIC FIELD

FIGURE 4. A Partial Representation of the Aesthetic Field as the Object of Criticism.

informed response. He also functions as a researcher into the experience of art who is adept at analyzing and assessing it. Let me explore this by turning to the behavior of critics and examining the relation of their observations to the aesthetic field.

PERCEPTION AND CRITICISM

The critic has a relationship to art that differs significantly from the aesthetic perceiver's. It is a difference that results from a marked dissimilarity in their activities, and it expresses itself in a characteristically distinct attitude. The experience of the appreciative observer is the primarily perceptual participation in the aesthetic field which we call aesthetic experience. He adopts an attitude that allows him to engage in the perceptually direct and unreflective experience of aesthetic value. The critic *qua* critic, on the other hand, engages in an intellectual activity which involves a substantially different process and requires a distinctly different attitude. Unlike the perceiver, the critic undertakes to examine this experience cognitively, and consequently the critical attitude is one of deliberate and careful reflection on the transactional experience of the field.

Thus while the perceiver in an aesthetic situation may be said to engage in *aesthetic valuing,* the critic as critic is concerned with the quite different function of *aesthetic evaluation.* The critic, therefore, is not a participant in the aesthetic field; rather he stands outside it. As a critic he is not part of the qualitative perceptual situation but instead takes this field as his subject matter and, at one remove from it, directs his critical faculties to conceptualizing, clarifying, and discriminating its perceptual qualities. Thus the critic notices relationships, draws comparisons, and abstracts features which occupy a significant role in the experience of a particular object. He engages, then, in a cognitive process directed toward the goal of arriving at propositional knowledge about the experience of art.

All this involves a duality of roles that requires of the critic a certain nimbleness. For, it is true, the critic begins as a perceiver. Yet to be effective as a critic, he must forsake his involvement to comment upon it, all the while retaining a vivid perceptual memory of the experience. The critic who gushes onto paper a verbal translation of his emotional responses never succeeds in making the transition from perception to reflection, and the bathos of impressionistic criticism makes us wonder at the critic rather than with him. Yet even when the critic finds his way from the participation with art in order to view it with detachment, he has a hard job to keep from emulating the artistic license of the poet and vying with him on aesthetic grounds. Critical literature is replete with examples of only partial success.

In contrast to the valuing that is part of the experience of art, then, critical activity reflects upon aesthetic experience. In pursuing this end, the critic combines, almost always implicitly, a theory of aesthetic value with a philosophy of criticism to arrive at his immediate goal—a judgment about the value of an art object.

THE ROLE OF CRITICISM

Yet this is not the critic's main function in the world of aesthetic activity. As I have already suggested, evaluation is but one phase of the full contribution of criticism. For criticism helps lay bare the intimate transaction that occurs within the aesthetic field and which involves the creation of art, the qualitative and structural features of the art object, and the perceptual response to it. As an accomplished and acute perceiver, the critic can show how creative techniques, decisions, and influences, how the art object which is their product, and how attitude and perceptiveness all combine to contribute to the final full experience of art. Thus the critic employs his skill, knowledge, and experience as an aesthetic percipient to function primarily as an instructor in the experience of art, assisting others in attaining a fuller perceptual experience by increasing the scope and intensity of aesthetic awareness. We can agree with Bosanquet that "the true critic, indeed, is he, and he only, who can teach us rightly to enjoy."[2]

---

[1] Note omitted.
[2] Bernard Bosanquet, *Three Lectures on Aesthetic*, Lecture I.

Consider what critics write about. They may construct a setting for our experience of the art object by noting the individuality of its place in the *history* of the art, how it relates to earlier art, and how it influenced that which followed. For example, one's perceptual awareness of Beethoven's Third Symphony, the "Eroica," is increased when one becomes attentive to those features by which it represents a major development of the symphonic form as it was used in the past. Such things as sheer magnitude, complexity of thematic development, elevation of the coda into a major formal division, the combination of a funeral march with the imaginative use of variation form—all these make the Eroica distinctive, and the critic can enhance our listening by calling attention to them so that they enter more fully into our perceptual field. Analogous literary examples might be the innovations in the novel that were represented by *The Remembrance of Things Past* and *Ulysses*.

Critics may also take note of the *circumstances* of an art work's creation. They may point out the formal or material restrictions of an art at a particular time that are imposed by the artist, specified by those who may commission the work, or required by its occasion or setting. It is appropriate to consider all these to the extent that they direct the perceiver's attention to noteworthy features of an art object. There is a similar value in the critical observation of cultural influences and national stylistic features. Thus the technical characteristics of the Baroque organ are germane to the kinds of tonal combinations appropriate to Bach's organ works, and the inability to execute dynamic shading on the harpsichord creates a characteristic interpretive feature of block-like dynamic contrast between sections of a composition written for that instrument. Likewise, the fact that techniques were not yet available for simulating distance through linear perspective in the graphic art of the thirteenth century imposed certain restrictions, just as the technical innovations of cubism eliminated others. Physical features of an artist's materials, like the invention of oil paints or the peculiar properties of a block of wood or stone (as in the marble used by Michelangelo for *David*) influence the planning of an artist and the decisions he makes in the course of executing a work. And biographical influences are too well known to warrant illustration. Our perceptual awareness is significantly enhanced, then, when the critic brings such information as this into play, as long as it is appropriate to the work being discussed and can increase our sensitivity to aspects of the object we might otherwise have overlooked. Its sole aesthetic justification lies in heightening aesthetic delight.

Probably most characteristic, though, is the attention critics give to the *intrinsic features* of an art object or an artistic performance. Character development in a novel, pacing in a dramatic presentation, composition in a painting, rhyme, meter and imagery in a poem—these are but a few of the many structural and perceptual features of which critics regularly take account. Moreover, because of the accepted importance of intrinsic criticism, these features are not only often taken to be the proper object of criticism; they are held to provide direct and sole support for critical evaluation. Yet as with the activities already mentioned, the value of the critic lies in the contribution he can make to aesthetic perception. By his ability to be sensitive to the perceptually relevant characteristics of an art object, the critic can direct the attention of the perceiver to subtle or neglected features, and so add to the perceptual richness of our appreciation. To do this, though, he must, like Baudelaire, forego locking himself up within " the blinding fortress of his system" in order to preach there at his ease. "A system is a kind of damnation which forces one to a perpetual recantation; it is always necessary to be inventing a new one, and the drudgery involved is a cruel punishment." Like Baudelaire, the critic must approach art with an "impeccable naiveté" and "resign [himself] to modesty."[3]

THE CONTRIBUTION OF THE CRITIC

When we view the activity of criticism in a broad perspective, then, we can see beyond the limits imposed by the critic's nominal task of judging the merits of an art object. We discover that criticism, especially by an informed and sensitive observer,

---

[3] Jonathan Mayne, *Baudelaire's Art Criticism* (Phaidon Press), 2 Vols.

has a unique and important place in the world of art. The critic is, in fact, an instructor in aesthetic perception.[4] If some critics are petty and bigoted, this is not a comment on their function but rather on their occasional failure to execute it properly. The good critic, however, prepares us for perception. He tells us what to look for so that we can savor the qualities and grasp the perceptual range of the object to a fuller extent. And he is informative to the extent that he is perceptually acute and intellectually astute. Thus the most difficult but most valuable service the critic can render is to lead us to an aesthetic perception of works that are difficult to approach, either because they are very new, old and forgotten, or come out of a culture that is foreign to the observer.[5] Further, the critic's judgments about the aesthetic value of an art object act as guides to and in aesthetic experience. They are instruments for ordering and interpreting such experience and they are also predictions of its quality and success.

This last point has a highly significant consequence. Because the judgments of the critic are predictions of the way in which an art object functions in the aesthetic field, they can be verified by the extent to which they lead to similar aesthetic experience for the art public that engages the object in relevant and full awareness. What this means is that art criticism is not the private domain and personal privilege of the critic, but rather that his judgments are subject to a common standard for determining their validity—the concurrence or lack of it among all those who have also experienced the art object in a full and intelligent way. And this means that it is the informed audience of any such object, instructed and influenced though it may be by the critic, that is the real judge of its merits.

Because of the economics of artistic success, the critic can and often does exercise a considerable influence on whether a painter sells or whether a theatrical production is a box office

---

[4] A notable instance of the educational influence of criticism is the pervasive effect the New Criticism has had on the teaching of poetry, although the New Critics tend to confuse their educational role with a judicial one.

[5] Cf. Victorino Tejera, *Art and Human Intelligence* (New York, Appleton-Century-Crofts, 1965), p. 165.

success.[6] Yet critics have been disregarded here, too, and in the long run they themselves are judged, together with the works they would evaluate, by the response of those they would lead. Rather than acting independently of public reaction, at his best the critic anticipates and exemplifies it. And if he does not succeed in doing this, he is not so much wrong as irrelevant. What is most surprising is that even critics themselves are beginning to discover this.[7]

When criticism is seen to revolve around aesthetic experience, it becomes possible to give an unstrained explanation of changes in critical judgment and, more particularly, of changes in tastes. No art is eternal, but the active use of art objects varies with the ability of an object, or, more generally, of a style, to get through to the perceiver and make contact with him in the direct immediacy of aesthetic experience. In most cases, this ability gradually declines until the object or style is perceptually effective only to one who has developed an uncommon familiarity with the art of a particular period. Changes in language, custom, belief all have an effect on this. Who now reads the late medieval romance but the scholar or student? Who attends performances of twelfth century music but the musicologist? And who views Mesopotamian or perhaps ancient Egyptian art with aesthetic enjoyment but the art historian (and his students)? Moreover there are similar stylistic tributaries in every period since the Renaissance which are the special province of the scholar. And it is for similar reasons that in times of great innovation the perceptual accessibility of art is limited to those who have imbued themselves with the interests and idioms of the *avant garde* and thus are able to enjoy these objects for their artistic rather than their sensationalistic effects.

It is true, though, that styles and the objects that embody them vary in their ability to last. This results most likely from

---

[6] To regard reviews as "money reviews," as they are called, on the basis of whether they will sell the picture, is to treat them as factors in the economics of the art business, not in its aesthetics.

[7] See Walter Kerr, "The Era of the Critic Draws to a Close," *The New York Times*, Section D, May 21, 1967, pp. 1, 3.

their degree of success in incorporating the perennial experience of human life freshly, forcefully, and with a minimum of dependence on special knowledge, practices, effects, and cultural circumstances. The great ages of artistic creation have succeeded in doing this, while the intervening ones have not. Greek tragedy, Renaissance painting, Elizabethan drama illustrate the ability of some art to endure long and well, while Roman poetry, medieval verse narratives, Renaissance music, and Rococo art appear to exhibit the reverse. In much the same way, the reawakening of rich experience in the art of past periods results from a change in our interest and receptivity. And this change is in a direction which renders a public more responsive than before to a neglected phase of the past which is seen to resemble a newly emerging sensibility. This may help account for the great surge of popularity for Baroque music and for African sculpture during recent decades, and for other such "redis-coveries" of the art of past ages and distant cultures.

NORMS, STANDARDS AND RULES

Thus common standards of criticism in art can be based only on common experiences. That is why different cultural groups display differences in taste and in their criteria of judgment, and why applying cross-cultural standards so often fails. All the elements in the aesthetic field are variable, since all are affected by the changes that take place in human social experience. The evolution of a culture, of society, technology, and ideology generate effects on the artist, the perceiver, the performer, and the object, as well as on the critic. Yet there are forces making for stability in the field, too. These are the basic biological, psychological, social, and perhaps historical characteristics of men, the sensory, ideational, intuitive resemblances in the quality of experience and the common physical influences and limitations on art objects. Such forces help produce a generic similarity in aesthetic experience and provide the only basis for common standards and judgments. Still, all these factors permit wide differences in taste and judgment. It would seem that the human element rather than the object is the source of differences in response and hence in judgment, and this is the reason often given for the impossibility of formulating universal principles of taste.[8] Yet this is only partially the case. For since the aesthetic field is a perceptual whole in which all the arts are elements in experience, the same forces that make for constancy and variability affect every aspect of the field.

All these sources of change and stability are mirrored by the norms and standards that are part of the critical armory. Aesthetic norms are notoriously impermanent, more so, often, than the very art they would judge. Instead of rules being the arbiters of art, art is actually the arbiter of rules. Norms in art express the aesthetic sensibility of the age, and they are extrapolated from those objects that function successfully and regularly in the aesthetic field. Hence they are always after the fact and unable to adapt easily to artistic novelty. What is valuable art is the result of aesthetic success, and what is relevant in criticism is thus determined by the art and not by the critic. Art, indeed, generates its own criteria for criticism, and as art evolves, so too must criticism. Nothing is more futile than attempting to apply Aristotle's standards for Greek tragedy to modern drama, Boileau's neoclassic adaptation of Aristotle and Horace to off-Broadway, or Baroque conventions against voice-leading in parallel fifths to music of the French impressionists. New art is always condemned by old rules, or, to be more precise, old rules are regularly disproved by new art.[9]

There is a mode of critical judgment related to the use of norms and rules that embodies the same disabilities. It is what

---

[8] Cf. Kant: "By a principle of taste I mean a principle under the condition of which we could subsume the concept of an object and thus infer, by means of a syllogism, that the object is beautiful. But this is absolutely impossible. For I must immediately feel pleasure in the representation of the object, and of that I can be persuaded by no grounds of proof whatever. Although, as Hume says, all critics can reason more plausibly than cooks, yet the same fate awaits them." *Critique of Judgment* (New York, 1951), p. 127.

[9] "We know that no norm owns such immortality, that most are like champions of the prize-ring; they have a life story of birth and growth, of battle for place and power, of a measure of victory and of final overthrow; that like others, they grow old and die a natural death. . . . The scope of a judgment of beauty is no greater than the range of the individuals who freely acquiesce in it and freely employ it. Their consent establishes its boundary." H. M. Kallen, *Art and Freedom* (New York, Duell, Sloan and Pearce, 1942), Vol. II, p. 960-961.

we might call *generic criticism,* judging art by style, by the extent to which an art object reflects or deviates from a style which one favors or condemns. Thus one may praise or blame a painting because it is cubist, abstract expressionist, or pop, or a musical work because it is serial, electronic, or tonal. Generic criticism makes a claim to orthodoxy that is not just the call of the traditionalist but is equally the demand of the innovator. Like critical rules, generic criticism is subsumptive. It overshadows the individuality of an art object with the universality of a type, and thus inverts the relation that emerges from the priority of aesthetic experience. Rules and stylistic classification do have a place, but not in the seat of judgment. They function rather as part of the scholarly apparatus for identifying similarities and lines of influence. Rules are the product of a descriptive analysis of what has already been done rather than prescriptive claims on what will be. We need critical analysis and order, but as a guide to our perception and understanding of the past instead of as a road into the artistic future. Thus standards and styles aid us as students of art and aesthetic perception rather than as artists or their judges. The validity of rules, then, is a cognitive validity, not an experiential one. Many standards do possess far-reaching applicability, and when they do it results from perceptual constants that these rules have succeeded in identifying. Yet as good art is constantly extending our perceptual range, so rules are constantly forced to modify themselves and adapt to new uses.

A CRITICAL HYPOTHESIS

Here, then, is an hypothesis about the function of criticism in the experience of art. It is intended as a description rather than a justification of the critical function, as an account of the actual role that criticism assumes in the broad range of artistic activity. Instead of seeing the critic's function as one of a judge, we recognize instead that it is that of an educator. The critic engages in what is basically a cognitive activity rather than a perceptual one, pointing out to us the characteristics of art objects, performances, artistic methods, and, most of all, the perceptual effects that these generate. Like the scholar, the critic stands outside the aesthetic field, inquiring into the experience of art and commenting on that experience. (See Fig. 5.)

Yet the critical inquiry originates in the aesthetic experience of the critic and leads, in turn, to the experience of his reader. Thus the critic's function is a circular one. Drawing upon his own valuational experience of art, he is able to make an informed and illuminating description of his encounter with particular art objects. Not only does he describe their characteristics; he also identifies their relationships with one another and interprets the significance of the entire field in the larger region of human life. When he does this successfully, the critic informs and instructs us, aiding us in achieving a fuller, truer, more rewarding experience of the work. (See Fig. 6.)

This account, however, does not assign a primarily judicial function to the critic, and this is deliberate. For to center criticism on an evaluative role not only shifts it away from the function it actually performs; it deprives of recognition the real holder of that role. Effective judgment in art is in fact educated, collective concurrence by the art public with whom art works. It is this that is the beginning and end of styles as well as of particular objects. As artists and critics are part of the art public, so they contribute to the process of evaluation. But as they are only parts of that public, they do not determine it.[10]

Thus are criticism and judgment distinct. Criticism, although deprived of a judical function, does indeed perform a valuable task. For as an educational activity, criticism mediates between the past experiences on which critical judgments are based and future experiences through which their validity is constantly reconsidered and genuine conclusions about aesthetic merit achieved. Through such a mediating activity, the criticism of art plays two vital roles: It instructs its audience in achieving fuller perceptual awareness, and by assisting the art public in attaining

----

[10] There is a public standard of criticism implicit in the French practice of putting paintings into the Luxembourg Museum for fifty years, and then either placing them in the Louvre or throwing them out!

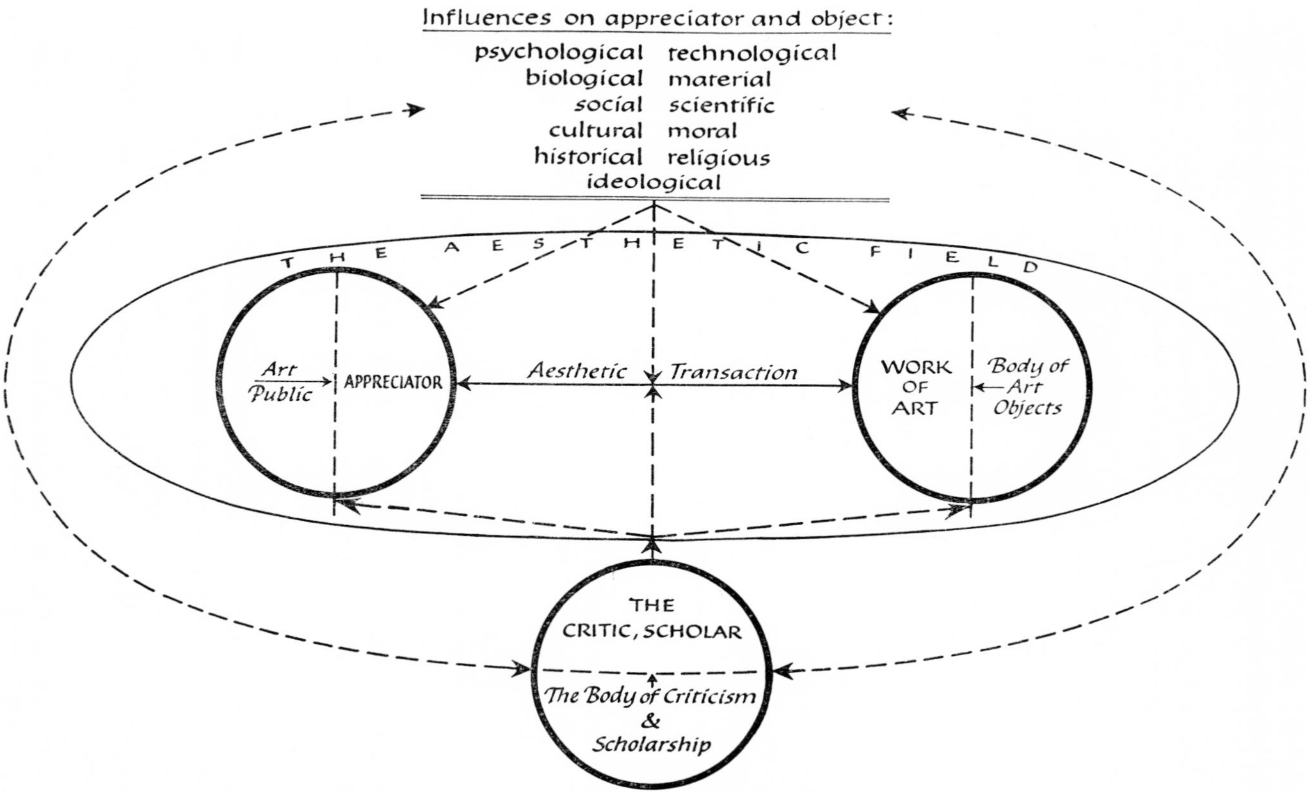
Influences on appreciator and object:
psychological technological
biological material
social scientific
cultural moral
historical religious
ideological
THE AESTHETIC FIELD
Art Public
APPRECIATOR
Aesthetic Transaction
WORK OF ART
Body of Art Objects
THE CRITIC, SCHOLAR
The Body of Criticism & Scholarship

FIGURE 5. The Relationships of the Critic to the Aesthetic Field.

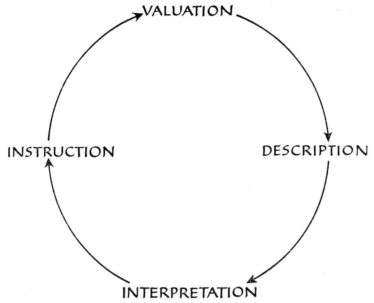

FIGURE 6. The Critical Function.

a common store of aesthetic experience, it lays the groundwork for a common body of aesthetic judgment.

AESTHETIC VALUE

We come, finally, to the issue which it is usual to regard as the central one in art, the nature and basis of aesthetic value. Yet as must now be apparent, aesthetic value is not the major premise of an empirical aesthetics but rather one of its theorems. Still it will be asked, how can we determine aesthetic value, and how do standards for judgment grow out of descriptive and explanatory accounts? In approaching these questions, Hanslick pointed the way a century ago: "The whole course of the present inquiry never approaches the question of what *ought to be,* but simply of what *is.* We can deduce from it no definite ideal of the truly beautiful in music, but it enables us to show what is equally beautiful even in the most opposite styles."[11]

---

[11] Eduard Hanslick, *The Beautiful in Music* (1854) (Indianapolis, Bobbs-Merrill, 1957), p. 62.

Let me begin by drawing a basic and important distinction, one which follows from what we have observed about aesthetic perception and criticism. This is the difference between the *valuational experience* of art and the *evaluative* or *critical judgments* we make about such experience. To speak of the experience of art as valuational is to identify one aspect of that experience as it is actually had. The very experience is valuable— value is not something added to it or derived from it. This, however, is not the case with evaluative judgments. These are the cognitive products of inquiry into art and deliberation over it. As such, evaluation is a different order of thing, and like all cognitive judgments, it is controversial in varying degrees.

If aesthetic experience is primary, then aesthetic value corresponds to the degree to which such experience is most complete and functions most successfully. There is, to be sure, a certain circularity here, yet it is more an apparent circularity than a vacuous one. It might seem as though the successful experience of art provides the criteria for our analysis of aesthetic experience, and that the more closely our experience fulfills these criteria the more aesthetic value it possesses. Hence, standards of value are implicit in the initial identification of the successful experience of art.

This, however, is both trivial and false. It is trivial because successful experience of art *is* valuational experience, and so the description of such experience possesses from the outset a certain normative element. Value is not something superadded to art; it is rather an intrinsic dimension of our relationship to it. It is moreover false to claim circularity here, because the valuational experience of art is not identical with evaluative judgment, and such judgment is the product of that experience, not its source. Thus the relation between aesthetic experience and aesthetic judgment is not a circular but rather an inferential one. Aesthetic judgment is dependent but not assumptive. It is the cognitive product of the examination of our aesthetic encounter and embodies the results of that inquiry, not its subject matter. Aesthetic value, however, is there in any case, to be recognized, to be experienced, to be formulated, but not to be constituted.

THE FUNCTION OF AESTHETIC EXPERIENCE

The richness of an art object, we have noted, is the basis on which its value rests. It is the potential ability of that object to function successfully in the aesthetic field. What such functioning is I have already examined in some detail, yet there is one aspect that has so far remained unexplored. That is the functional relation of the field as a whole to the broader context of human life.

Despite the frequency with which the claim is made for artistic autonomy, for the complete freedom and independence of the artist, there have been just as frequent challenges. Moreover, not all these challenges have come from the philistine or the ideologue. The artist himself has sometimes insisted that his work has a relevance that extends beyond the boundaries of the object. Yet there are really two things here, and they are not incompatible. There is the matter of *freedom from control over art,* one of the more important conditions for successful productivity. Then there is the matter of *freedom for influence by art,* the real contribution of the arts to a civilization and a contribution that is diminished when it is restricted by official censorship or social prohibitions. Nor is special pleading involved here. It is rather the request that the artist and his art be allowed to fulfill its function fully and freely.

For although art is worthwhile in itself, it does not exist for its own sake. Art does in fact break the bindings of books, stretch beyond the framed canvas, and leap off the stage to invade our lives at every turn. The seclusion of art is not a triumph of refinement but rather a cultural restriction on the full range of its effectiveness. Art does permeate every corner of our lives, however. Rather than restricting the artist and controlling his work by keeping it out for pornographic or political reasons or by keeping it in for reasons of acquisition and protection, we ought first to recognize the pervasiveness of the artistic contribution to culture and then promote it.

What is this contribution? What, in other words, is the larger role of aesthetic experience? It is sometimes said that art has the job of teaching us something.[12] This is not necessarily to teach us that anything is or is not so, but rather how to do something better, like see grass or hear the sounds of night. Yet what we *learn* from art is one of the *consequences* of aesthetic experience. It is not, however, its function. This function is rather to give us the opportunity to experience; no, more than this, it is to *be* experience itself, more fully, more intensely, more purely, and with greater qualitative subtlety and variety than in any other situation. To the extent that worship, sport, and sociality to do this, to that extent do they merge with art. We all have our memories of rare but rich hours when we entered into the beautiful, the tragic, and the whole range of living between and beyond these, times which are indistinguishable from occasions of high art. Aesthetic experience is but life lived most richly, most completely. To that extent it is not apart from life, an escape from life. Life, on most occasions, is rather an escape from art; it is usually alienated from itself.

Education may be regarded as a process of coming to self-consciousness, of both discovering and creating ourselves as we participate in the unending activity of acculturation. In a similar fashion, aesthetic education is a process of developing self-awareness of experience, in its sensory, imaginative, and social dimensions. Thus the role of art is not teaching but it is nonetheless educational. It neither imparts nor communicates, but rather joins with us in an activity of disclosure. Thus can Cassirer say, "It is not the degree of infection but the degree of intensification and illumination which is the measure of the excellence of art."[13] The value of art, then, lies directly in its functional relation to human life, in its ability to expand, enhance, and enrich the qualitative dimensions of all experience. Although such experience is not evaluative, it is nonetheless valuational, and therefore we can formulate judgments on the basis of the ability of art to sustain and develop such a relationship.

----

[12] Cf. J. H. Randall, Jr. *Nature and Historical Experience* (New York, Columbia University Press, 1958), p. 282.

[13] Ernst Cassirer, *Essay on Man*, p. 189. Cf. also Lewis Mumford, *Technics and Civilization*, p. 76.

ART AND VALUE

I come, finally, to the main philosophical issue in this discussion, the question of the kind of value that art has. Here we must bring to bear the results of our analysis, for there are several different questions to consider, and each reqiures a different kind of answer. The first is, What is the value *in* aesthetic experience? As we have seen, it is possible to develop an answer to this by an empirical inquiry that is directed toward clarifying valuational experience as it actually occurs in the situations in which we engage with art objects, that is, in the aesthetic field. A second question is, What is the value *of* aesthetic experience? Probing this question actually involves examining the valuational dimension of the aesthetic field. Having identified the presence of aesthetic value, what are its characteristics? How does it relate to the other modes of valuational experience which men have? There is yet a third question that is implicated in any answer to the second, but, derivative though it is, it is usually taken as the main issue. This is the question, What is the value of art (in the sense of the art object)? These are, to be sure, broad and difficult questions, yet it is possible to make some meaningful and constructive suggestions toward answering them.

Let me begin with the first of these, the question of the value *in* aesthetic experience. One of the points that emerged from the analysis of aesthetic experience in the last chapter was that the experience of art calls forth intrinsic perception. As experience, art is qualitatively self-sufficient; it is complete and final. Yet this is a comment on perceptual experience. What, however, can one say about the value that inheres in such experience?

It will help to recall the distinction between aesthetic experience and aesthetic judgment, between the actual encounter with art and the product of our reflective deliberation on that encounter. Applied to the problem of aesthetic value, we can distinguish aesthetic valuing, the valuational experience of art (what Dewey calls "prizing"), from aesthetic evaluation, the normative judgment of art (Dewey's "appraising"). At this point a most interesting observation can be made. It is that *value as experienced is always intrinsic,* in the sense of being had directly in and of itself. Valuational experience is simply there in the contextual event, and all experience is valuationally intrinsic. As it is had, it is neither discriminated nor is it judged. It simply is. Moreover, our experience with art is a paradigm case of intrinsic valuing. Art does not lead us to experience. It *is* experience, primary experience, whose valuational qualities are as inseparable a part of the unity of that experience as any of its other perceptual qualities are. The valuational dimension of listening to Berg's *Violin Concerto* or seeing Grünewald's *Crucifixion* is as inherent a part of those occasions as it is of eating hot buttered popcorn. What is different, however, is the multifaceted, broadly inclusive and highly intensified quality of the typical situation in which we encounter art. But a hungry man would see it differently, of course.

To say that value occurs as an inherent part of human experience, and therefore that aesthetic value is an inseparable part of aesthetic experience, identifies the locus of valuation. When we raise the question of the value *of* aesthetic experience, the value that the aesthetic field possesses, however, we pursue quite a different matter. Here we are talking about an analytic object, not an experiential one, and the question of value consequently becomes a judgmental question. When we stand back and observe the activity of art, we discover that there is a full and constant interchange between the aesthetic encounter and the entire range of active human experience. Art does not exist in Olympian isolation: In a vacuum there is no sound; without light there is no color; without an aesthetic perceiver there is no art but merely senseless physical events. And men, as creatures of circumstance, take their art with them out of the concert hall and the gallery into the human traffic of daily life, just as they bring themselves as worldly creatures to their art. Thus as an integral part of the activity of that cultural animal we call man, art participates in the network of human involvements with the natural and social environment, drawing inspiration from it and feeding an enlightened perception and increased sensitivity back into it.

To *judge* the value of art, then, is to recognize its inextricable ties to human activity and therefore its place in the pattern of means and goals in which men are immersed. Thus we have to take account of the causal network in which the aesthetic field functions. I have already explored some of the ways in which a wide variety of social, cultural, organic, and technical factors influence the experiential qualities of particular aesthetic fields.[14] What aestheticians have recognized somewhat less commonly is the powerful action of aesthetic experience as a causal force in its own right. The moralist is not mistaken in accusing the arts of being a threat to established practices and conventional sensibility. He is rather misguided in judging this to be wrong or improper. For art is a creative force in the social order. It is a source of new experience; it is, in fact, the education of experience in its most direct and unencumbered form.

Yet the relation of art to experience is not mainly a derivative relationship, once removed from the involvement with art. Art is rather a primary mode of experience which both feeds into and helps form other modes. Effective art is always radical, returning us to our roots in direct experience so that our involvement becomes more authentic. This, in fact, is the ultimate test of aesthetic value. When we engage with great art we become spiritually naked—all falsity, pretense, and affectation are revealed for what they are. This is not only true of new art but of effective art from past traditions as well. Yet there is a special contribution that contemporary art is able to make. For the significant contemporary artistic work in any period is that which identifies and reveals the sensibility of that age, and it is therefore likely to be most penetrating and reconstructive at that time.[15] This helps us understand, too, the regular shifts in style and fashion. These changes are demanded by the very same need for constant perceptual stimulation and variety as we can observe in the history of the so-called practical arts like dress, cooking, and manners. Not only are all the regions of art directly affected by new discoveries in material, medium, and technique; they also respond to the need to rejuvenate our

---

[14] See Chapter III, above.

[15] I. A. Richards, for example, has connected artistic success with ordering ordinary experience in a strikingly original way.

perceptual interest. Thus the experience of the arts educates our sensibilities, making us more discriminating and aware. It changes the ways in which we look at ourselves and at others, affecting our sympathies and forcing us to reestablish our values on firmer, truer ground.

There are two extremely interesting consequences to this analysis of the value of art. One is that we must relinquish the common belief that the art object is the isolated possessor of intrinsic value, a pure refuge from the crassness and ugliness of the practical world. Art can not be set apart to be honored or avoided. It is neither precious and reserved for special occasions nor useless and quarantined. As part of the culture of man, art participates in the life of society, responding to its needs, its joys, and its despairs, and forcing us to meet and incorporate them into the very quality of our being. Recognizing this, we come to realize that *the value of art as judged is always instrumental.* Art, as an activity in the natural-social world, participates in a causally endless and inclusive order of desires and needs, of actions and responses, and can thus be adequately judged only in relation to that order and in extrinsic terms. *Aesthetic value, then, is experienced as intrinsic and judged as extrinsic.*[16] (See Fig. 7.)

A second consequence for the value of art follows directly from the first. This is the breakdown of the distinction we are accustomed to drawing between the fine and the practical arts. If art must be regarded judgmentally as instrumental, then all art is practical in so far as it participates in the cultural life of man. What varies is the precise manner of its participation, and it is only in this regard that we can discover meaningful differences. Consider the variety of ways in which intrinsic

---

[16] See the very useful discussion by Monroe C. Beardsley, "Intrinsic Value," (*Philosophy and Phenomenological Research*, XXVI, 1 (Sept. 1965), 1-17. Beardsley constructs a convincing case against intrinsic value, developing certain leads found in Dewey. Both Beardsley and Dewey, however, do not draw a clear distinction between the two quite different activities of experiencing value (i.e. valuing) and judging value (i.e. evaluating), even though it is implicit in their arguments, thereby obscuring their case somewhat. See also Dewey's *Art as Experience*, pp. 139, 198. I have developed this distinction in generalized form and in fuller detail in "The Experience and Judgment of Value," *Journal of Value Inquiry*, I (Spring 1967), pp. 24-37.

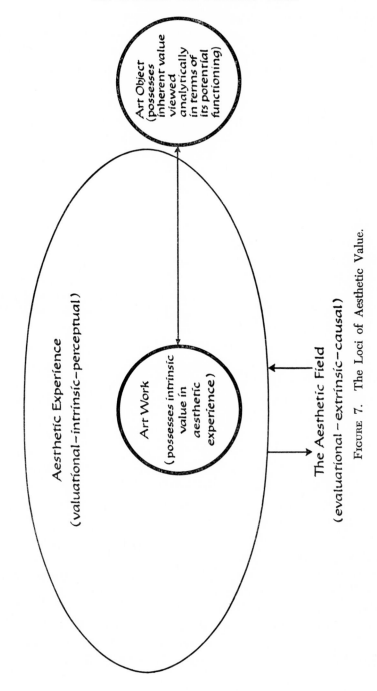

Figure 7. The Loci of Aesthetic Value.

perceptual qualities acquire extrinsic practical interests. In dance, free movement and significant gesture reawaken the biological vitality of the body. Dance takes physical actions from the harried confines of stiff and thoughtless movement and clarifies and purifies them through stylistic means so that we turn to the quotidian world chastened, refreshed, and more aware. Theater and film draw from the great variety of human situations; painting from the forms, tones, lines of the visual sphere; sculpture and architecture from the mass, planes, textures, space of our physical environment; music, the most inward of the arts, from time, sound, pulse and the bioconscious dynamic of life. Each art, in its own way, derives from the infinitely fertile matrix of perceptual experience and replenishes its source in an endlessly enriching cycle.

Yet the traditional discrimination of the fine from the practical arts is really a classification of art objects, and this leads to the last of the three questions, that of the value of these objects. Here we must ask whether the question is directed toward the object as it participates in aesthetic experience or toward the art object as an analytic constituent of the aesthetic field. In both cases, its value is derivative. In the first, the object is experienced as a locus of intrinsic value in the aesthetic encounter. The painting or the statue shares intrinsic value as an inseparable part of the aesthetic situation. In the second case, the object is *judged* valuable by the effectiveness with which it functions in the field. Through its ability in enabling us to realize intrinsic value in experience, it possesses inherent value, to use C. I. Lewis' term for this kind of extrinsic value. It is, then, causally related to the intrinsic valuing process in aesthetic experience, and as an object it must be judged as a reflected value by its functional success in the field. With this in mind, any object can figure in an aesthetic situation, just as it can in a moral one, and we judge it in such a light. Here the division between the fine and the practical enters and applies to the characteristic use of objects. Actually all objects in aesthetic experience are fine, and all objects in the aesthetic field are practical. We *judge* their value by their functional effectiveness, and hence the concept of function is the primary category in determining such value.

All objects are functional in this sense, and the distinction between the fine and the practical refers, insofar as it does not mislead us, to the extent to which an object or class of objects *typically* participates in the aesthetic field. When some objects are characteristically used in practical affairs rather than in aesthetic experience, we call them works of practical art, like tables, chairs, and tools. When they function regularly in aesthetic experience, we call them fine art, like the music and painting of high culture. Yet these functions are hardly inviolable. Moreover there are especially important arts of the present which do not fall neatly into either category, since their usual function is concurrently aesthetic and practical, and hence we do not know where to place them nor how to regard them. Architecture is one such art and film another. Both participate in quite different ways in the common life of contemporary culture with such intensity and pervasiveness that we cannot set them off in customary ways. And, of course, the common case of the practical objects of one culture becoming aesthetic objects of another culture or another age is familiar testimony to the fluidity of experiential contexts. "Practical" and "aesthetic," then, are epithets of setting and of use, and not properties of objects.[17]

Considered in this way, questions of aesthetic value can be pursued thoughtfully. They become empirical questions, allowing us to search for answers in behavioral experience or in causal relations. Aesthetic value is not impervious to analysis nor to the possibility of general agreement. As a central part of the valuational context of human life, artistic value is too important to be isolated and too significant to be unknown.

---

[17] Cf. A. Berleant, "Aesthetic Function," in *Phenomenology and Naturalism*, Dale Riepe (Ed.), forthcoming.

VI

TOWARD AN EMPIRICAL AESTHETICS

Here, then, is an alternative to the surrogate theories of art. It is an approach that proceeds by locating the reference of aesthetic theory in the aesthetic field. The significance of the art object, of the perceiver, of the creative artist and performer, and of the variety of biological, psychological, technological, historical, and cultural factors which affect an aesthetic event becomes clearer when we examine each element in the context of the active environment in which it assumes its characteristic aesthetic function. This is a proposal which maintains that the only legitimate grounds for elaborating a theoretical account of art lies in a clear, literal understanding of aesthetic experience, without recourse to either surrogate or metaphor. Thus it is a naturalistic aesthetic, one which "does not seek to discover the 'ultimate nature' of beauty" or transport our encounter with art to a transcendental realm. Rather it is content "to explore the experiences of beauty and its outer and inner concomitants on a phenomenal level.[1] It is an explanation which rests on a tentative description of such experience. Nine principal features of aesthetic experience emerged in this analysis, and each of them requires that we revise or reject traditional ways of accounting for art. It was described as experience that is active-receptive, qualitative, sensuous, immediate, intuitive, non-cognitive, unique, intrinsic and integral. When these features predominate as a group in an experiential situation, that experience takes on a prevailing aesthetic character.

This descriptive approach has also made it possible to handle the troublesome questions of art criticism more profitably.

------

[1] Thomas Munro, "Naturalism in Philosophy and Aesthetics," *J. of Aesthetics and Art Criticism*, XIX, p. 135.

Viewed in the light of his actual function, the critic is no longer the arbiter of art but an aesthetic educator instead. He makes a productive contribution in his own right to the social function of art as the awakener of sensibilities dulled by habit or disuse, and carries forward the humanizing work of the artist. Moreover, once we recognize how critical judgments rest on the success with which an art object functions in the field, we find that they then become open to verification by this empirical standard.

So, too, are questions of aesthetic value more tractable when we become less presumptuous through deferring to the natural locus of values and more confident through our ability to identify and use them. By distinguishing our valuational experience of art from our evaluative judgments, it is possible to recognize the authority of aesthetic value while retaining our claim to judge it by its own standards. Since the value in aesthetic experience is always intrinsic and the value of such experience always instrumental, we can admit the full cultural role of art while granting it the kind of autonomy that is essential for it to perform that role.

Should this phenomenology of aesthetic experience be accurate, a number of interesting consequences for our understanding of art follow. Some of these suggest that common explanations of the nature of art—views I have described as surrogate theories since they offer dependent interpretations of art as imitation, form, emotion, communication, or expression—must either be completely reconstructed and reinterpreted, or else entirely rejected. Other consequences involve the rejection of traditional aesthetic doctrines and beliefs, such as assigning truth to art, adopting an attitude for appreciation that removes the perceiver to a distance or places the object in isolation, replacing the sensory aspects of the experience with intellectual ones, eternalizing the art object, substituting symbol for sense and form for perception, and relegating art to a secluded haven that is private and subjective.

In place of surrogate theories and misleading doctrines, a view of art emerges that conceives of art as an activity of a considerably different sort. It is an activity that solicits an involved, responsive receptivity in the appreciation of art, a genuine participation in an experience of primary, qualitative perception. Here there is a fusion of sense, imagination, and intense awareness, an acceptance of the validity of sensual appeal, a homogeneity of the senses in an original, thoroughly creative act. With the rejection of acquired inhibitions comes an openness to all the facets of unmediated experience, where everything, including the objects and actions of everyday life, possesses aesthetic potential. It is the rediscovery of the uniqueness and originality of experience, of its intrinsic properties and its perceptual integrity, and finally of the continuity between the aesthetic and the nonaesthetic that leads ultimately to a harmony of experience for man in society and for man in his world. There is, further, the recognition of the valuational character of the experience of art, a character which opens art to critical reflection and enables us to determine its value as experience in its own right and at the same time to judge its place in the scheme of human goods.

All this is only a partial exploration of what follows from accepting a thoroughly empirical methodology for aesthetic theory. It is but a tentative indication of the shape of an aesthetics that emerges from a phenomenology of aesthetic experience. While the precise content of such a theory has yet to be developed, its implications, as we have seen, are nonetheless clear and unambiguous. We must remove the crutch of surrogate theories, subtracting such metaphorical ascriptions to the aesthetic event as "true-to-life," "resembles," "symbolizes," "means," "communicates," "expresses," and the rest of the pack of cognitive or linguistic epithets. We must leave off all claims to truth and its counterfeit, illusion. We must drop the ancient dualistic or trinitarian psychology that sees emotion as an exclusive alternative to reason or impulse. We must discard all moral, cultural, and historical prohibitions and expectations. We must acknowledge that art is presentational rather than representational, immediate rather than mediate, perceptual rather than conceptual, unique rather than abstract, intuitive and contextual rather than analytic and fragmented, and above all, neither cognitive, inferential, nor discursive. Finally, we must admit the full range of direct, undifferentiated human involvement. Only then will the actual scope of aesthetic experience begin to emerge and its overwhelming significance for the enrichment of human life become clear. Freed from the restrictions of being confined to an art object or to the spiritual flexings of an esthete, aesthetic experience will be recognized as having a primary place in the life of man as its original source and final culmination.

I have tried to trace a true path through the maze of aesthetic surrogates and back to the direct authenticity of our engagement with art. Whatever the difficulties with the theory I have outlined here, I hope that it has at least one virtue—that its contentions can be confirmed or disproved by empirical investigation. Such a theory has innumerable implications for inquiry in the behavioral sciences, suggesting directions in which we can increase our store of aesthetic facts about aesthetic perception, valuational experience, art objects, and all the factors that condition the aesthetic field. This, therefore, is not a task for the aesthetician alone; it requires the cooperation of the philosopher, the historian, and the many behavioral scientists whose work bears on the artistic activities of men.

The views I have proposed, then, are intended to suggest directions more than answers. This book does not offer a position to be disputed only dialectically. By claiming to account for aesthetic experience, it must therefore be tested against such experience. It can end, then, in no better way than by proposing a beginning.

INDEX

DATE DUE

GAYLORD

PRINTED IN U.S.A.